Golf

Getting to the Next Level

Golf

Getting to the Next Level

Brian Ferreira

NH
NEW
HOLLAND

First published in 2006 by

New Holland Publishers

London • Cape Town • Sydney • Auckland

www.newhollandpublishers.com

86 Edgware Rd
London W2 2EA
United Kingdom

80 McKenzie Street
Cape Town 8001
South Africa

14 Aquatic Drive
Frenchs Forest,
NSW 2086
Australia

218 Lake Road
Northcote, Auckland
New Zealand

Publishing managers: Claudia Dos Santos,
Simon Pooley

Commissioning editor: Alfred LeMaitre

Editor: Katja Splettstoesser

Designer: Elmari Kuyler

Illustrator: Steven Felmore

Picture researcher: Tamlyn Beaumont-Thomas,
Karla Kik

Proofreader/Indexer: Rod Baker

Production: Myrna Collins

Consultant: Traviss Willcox

ISBN: 1 84537 297 2 (HB);
         1 84537 301 6 (PB)

Reproduction by Resolution Colours (Pty) Ltd,
Cape Town, South Africa

Printed and bound in Malaysia by Tien Wah
Press (Pte) Ltd

2 4 6 8 10 9 7 5 3 1

Contents

chapter 1

Introduction

Golf is a game of endless challenges and amazing rewards. It does appear to be fairly straightforward when watching good golfers play, but it's not as easy as it looks. Unfortunately, that's why many beginners give up within the first few months of starting the game and never get to experience its pleasures.

As with everything in life, we need goals and challenges; we need to test our ability to keep going when times are hard. From the first time we swing a club there are always areas in which we can better ourselves: we can try to hit a ball straighter and further, improve our score or hole more putts.

Regardless of our standards, we always have room to enhance our skills and when we do, the rewards are indescribable. The inner feeling of success, the satisfaction of knowing that we can do it and the incredible joy when we eventually get the ball to do exactly what we want it to – these are the reasons we persevere.

➲ *Golf is a game of precision. Careful attention to detail in all areas of the game is essential and can profoundly effect your overall performance.*

Practice makes perfect

It takes time and patience to build a good golf swing and to develop the correct frame of mind, but if you are prepared to spend some time understanding the basics of the swing, this game will give you enormous pleasure.

The problem is that most golfers never seek professional advice. They buy a set of clubs, go to the driving range a few times and rush out onto the course. A lot of them will give up within the first few months – embarrassed, frustrated and humiliated. I thought I was different. I wanted to be a good golfer and went to every golf pro I could find. I wanted to

learn how to hit a golf ball consistently well and make a good score; I got close. By the time I was 16 years old, I could score in the 60s and thought of myself as pretty good. Looking back now, I didn't have a clue – I would score 64 one day and 84 the next. Eventually I stopped playing because of the frustration. My yearning to hit a golf ball consistently well would not go away, however. My father was a good all-round sportsman and played a very good game of golf, getting down to about a two-handicap. Golf was in my blood and I wanted to get back into it. So I started teaching at a local driving range, and

every single person made precisely the same mistake every time. Even though the individual swings looked different, the basic causes of the bad shots were always the same.

Eventually it dawned on me: instinct was the cause. Every good shot we play in this game is as the result of an unnatural movement, but playing instinctively will cause a bad shot. Take, for example, the tendency among players to put their weight on their back feet during a golf swing and how they try to lift their club from behind. This only results in the low point in the arc of the club being behind the ball. By the time it strikes, the club swings upwards and catches the top half of the ball, imparting topspin. As a result, the ball scuttles along the ground and does not get airborne.

As in this case, very few of us give physics a second thought during our swing or even when we hit a golf ball. How often do we think about how we place our hands on the club, the way we take the club back and how we are about to play the ball?

Knowing why you hit bad shots is important. This will enable you to work against them and build new 'muscle memory'. Not only will your game improve, but so will your enjoyment of it. Learning to chip and putt reasonably well, getting the ball to fly straight and improving your score may be a huge challenge to overcome, but just a few hours of practice each week will have you seeing results in these areas, and the rewards will be immeasurable.

❶ *Developing self-confidence in golf can only be achieved through practice and perseverence.*

getting people to hit balls better than they had ever done before gave me enormous satisfaction.

Nevertheless, after hitting many balls in my time, playing countless rounds and teaching hundreds of people to play, I still did not know why I struggled so much with the golf swing. I knew that swinging across the target line with an open clubface would cause a slice, but why was it so difficult to stop doing it? After a few months at the range, I realized that

chapter 2

The Long Game

The long game is the term used for full shots, those from the tee to the fairway, or from the fairway to the green. An efficient long game enables you to keep the ball 'in play', avoiding the rough and the hazards along the way. Getting the ball onto the fairways and greens in regulation figures is obviously the ultimate goal, but history has shown us that no golfer has yet been able to consistently achieve 100% accuracy.

Your imagination, willpower and concentration will determine the quality of your golf shot, more so than your physical attributes. Accept the fact that you might not hit every shot perfectly and proceed from there. Think about the shots that you did not execute well and try to avoid the same mistakes.

You can overcome nervousness with positive thoughts; focus on getting the ball to your target and keep your swing smooth and balanced. Visualize the flight of the ball, feel the swing you need to produce and relax as much as possible.

➲ *Harness and focus your determination, imagination and willpower if you want to hit good shots consistently in a game of golf.*

Address

The address, also referred to by golfers as the setup, is the manner in which you align your body in relation to your target. When combined with an accurate aim, the address determines the path your ball will take.

The perfect aim

It might seem fairly simple, but setting up on the right line is difficult and is relative to the way you last hit the ball. If it went right of the target, you might overcompensate for this by aiming the ball left in the next shot, causing the club to fly through to the left of the target. This would then create another set of problems, as your body would be out of alignment and you would be unable to get your club through on the correct swing plane.

There is often pressure on the course to speed up play, but do not rush your set-up and alignment. Rather, get to your ball as soon as possible and give yourself a minute to get ready. Just a few seconds of real focus often makes the world of difference.

Try to get behind the ball and find a spot on the ground, about a foot or so ahead of the ball, in line with your target. Set up and point the club at that spot. Now get your feet and shoulders parallel to that target line. You can now be assured that you are aiming in the correct direction and are able to make a full, easy swing at the ball.

Ball position

For most shots, position the ball just ahead of your centreline so that you can hit it on the downswing while your club swings through on the target line. If you position it too far left then your shoulders will point left, causing the ball to take off in that direction. With the driver we need to hit the ball slightly on the upswing. In order to do this, position the ball further left in the setup, in line with your left heel. This gets the low point in the arc of the club just behind the ball and produces more roll when the ball hits the fairway. (Take care when setting up with the driver. Because the ball position is further left than with other clubs, it is a common fault among players to point their shoulders left of the target, which causes them to swing their club across the target line.)

The position of the ball when using a driver also means players need to delay hitting the driver a bit more than with other clubs. (Forcing and hitting too early in the downswing is the most common problem in golf.)

Positioning the ball

How you position the ball in relation to your feet is extremely important; place it so that you strike it on the downswing and swing with your club through on the target line. Ensure your posture and target alignment are correct.

The driver

For the driver, line up the ball with the heel of your left foot. This allows you to hit it on the upswing.

Long irons

With the long irons, position the ball just left of the centre-line. This will enable you to attack it at a flatter angle.

Short irons

With the short irons, position the ball in the centre of the feet. This will enable you to strike downward on the ball.

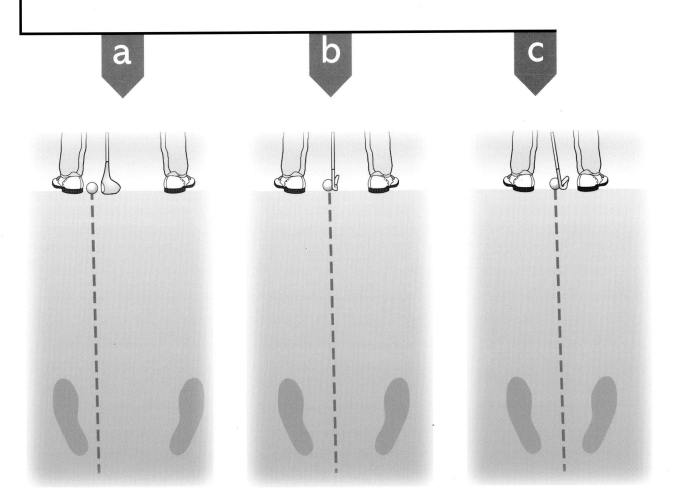

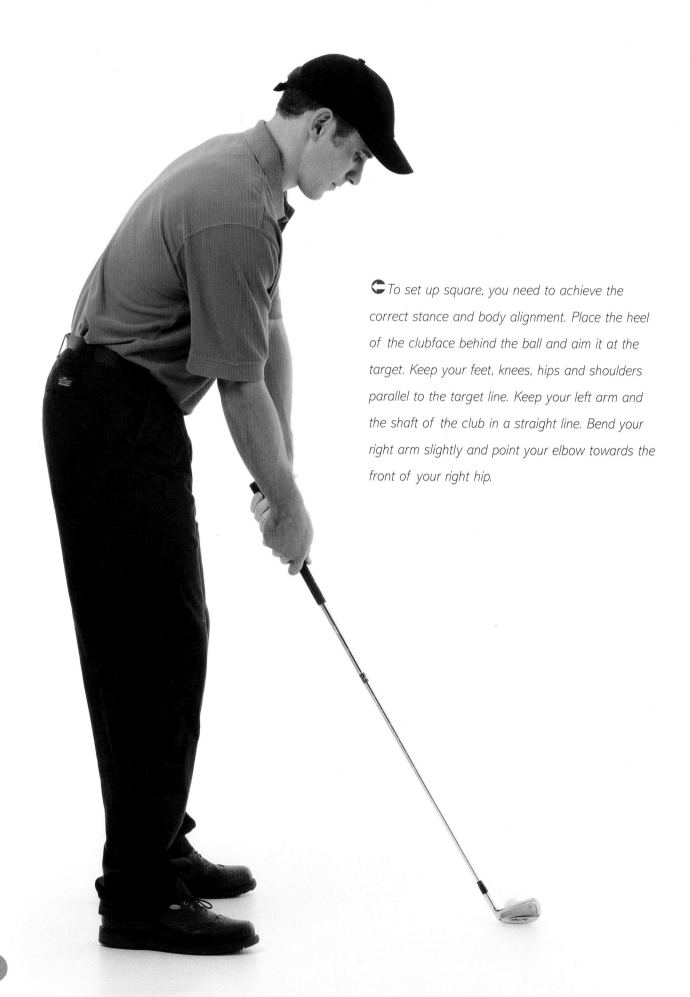

To set up square, you need to achieve the correct stance and body alignment. Place the heel of the clubface behind the ball and aim it at the target. Keep your feet, knees, hips and shoulders parallel to the target line. Keep your left arm and the shaft of the club in a straight line. Bend your right arm slightly and point your elbow towards the front of your right hip.

Clubface angles

1. A golfer who slices the ball (see p88) will instinctively place the club with its face pointing to the left. This make it very difficult to get the club back in the correct position.
2. The bottom or 'leading-edge' of the club must point to the target. Both the shaft of the club and the leading edge should be in a straight line.

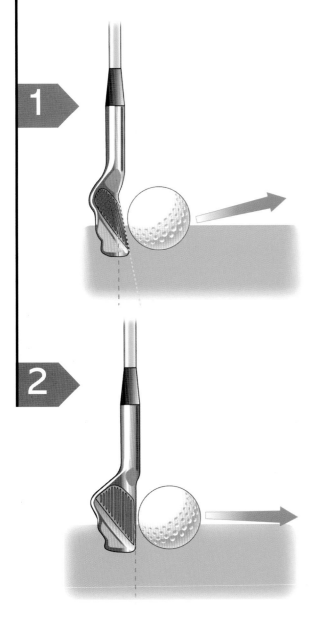

Club lies

1. When the club lie is too upright the ball will fly to the right.
2. When the toe of the club is off the ground the ball will fly to the left.
3. In a normal set-up position the sole of the club should lie flat on the ground.

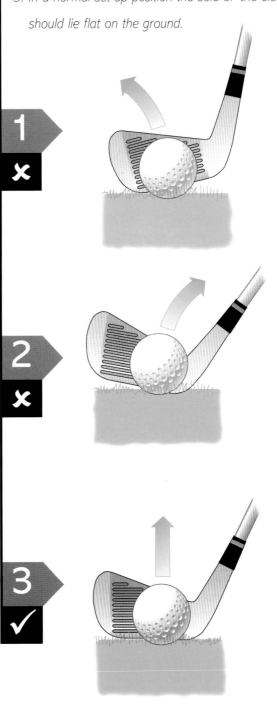

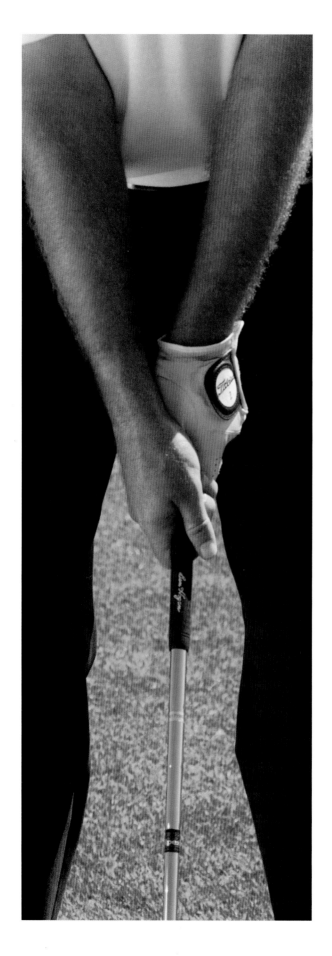

The grip

To build a good golf swing a good grip is essential. The position of your hands and your grip pressure on the club are absolutely vital components of the swing. To keep the club on the correct plane you need balance and flexibility to generate sufficient speed and keep the club on line.

The left hand

The left hand is vital to the overall effectiveness of your swing. If it collapses during the swing and the right hand gains control, you will hit a bad shot. The rubber handle on the club is thicker at the top than at the bottom, with very good reason.

The left hand must have a firm, solid hold at the top end of the club and your fingers, palm and thumb must fit in their entirety around its handle. If you see only one knuckle on the back of your left hand, you will probably hit the ball to the right, if you see four knuckles, you will probably hit the ball to the left. Seeing three knuckles is ideal.

The right hand

A balance of power between the left and right hands is needed in the grip. In order to achieve this balance, the strength of the right hand needs to equal that of the left. If the right hand overpowers the left at any stage in the swing, you will hit a bad shot, thus you need to regulate its strength. Because the rubber grip is thinner at its lower end, this encourages sole use of the fingers of the right hand. Do not touch the club with your palm and keep your right elbow close to your right hip. A very common error is to hold the club from the top of the grip, which causes the right shoulder to move forward and way out of position.

To adapt to the subsequent change in thinking that takes place when correcting a strong right-hand grip is a big adjustment. During the swing, you not only need to achieve balance between your left and right hands, but also the left and right halves of your body. This will enable you to hit the ball better.

For some reason, most beginners start off using an 'interlocking' grip, taking their left forefingers off their club and linking them with the small fingers of their right hand. I would suggest you rather go with the 'overlap' grip only, because taking your left forefinger off the club will weaken your left hand even more at a time when you really need to keep it as strong as possible.

Grip pressure

Weak grip

A grip is weak when you can only see one knuckle on the back of the left hand. This grip prevents you from rolling the club to the left and makes it easy for you to move the ball from left to right, or fade the ball (see p25).

Strong grip

Seeing four knuckles on the back of the left hand is indicative of a strong grip. Holding the club in this manner makes it easy for you to roll your hands in the hitting area and to draw the ball (see p25).

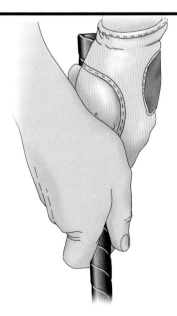

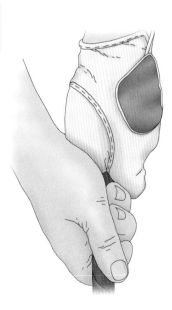

Grip formation

Your hands connect you to the club, and that connection needs to be correct. Very small changes in your grip can cause dramatic changes in the flight of the ball.

1. *Place the top end of the club across the joints of the fingers of the left hand.*

2. *Close the fingers around the club ensuring there are no gaps between them.*

3. *Wrap the palm over the top of the club, so that you can see three knuckles on the back of the left hand: those of the fore, middle and ring finger. You should not see the knuckle of the small finger. Your thumb should be on top of the club, lying slightly right of centre.*

4. *Using only your left hand, pick the club up in front of you. The grip pressure needed to keep the club there is what you require during the swing; just enough to know that the club will not twist in your hand while you are swinging. With the right hand, hold the club with the thumb, middle and ring fingers only, the fingertip of the middle finger touching the left side of the left thumb, and the ring finger touching the forefinger of the left hand.*

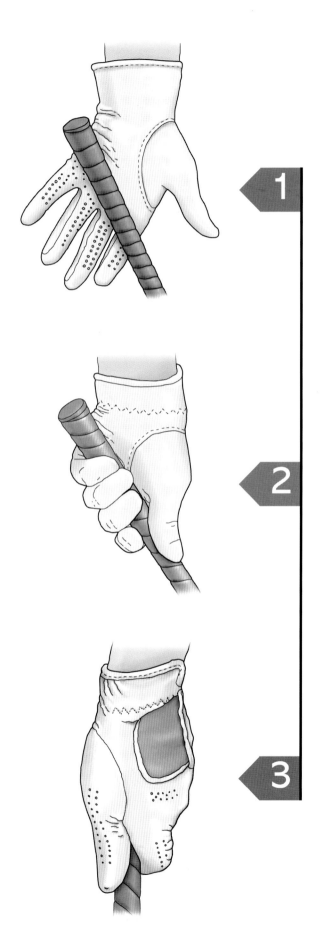

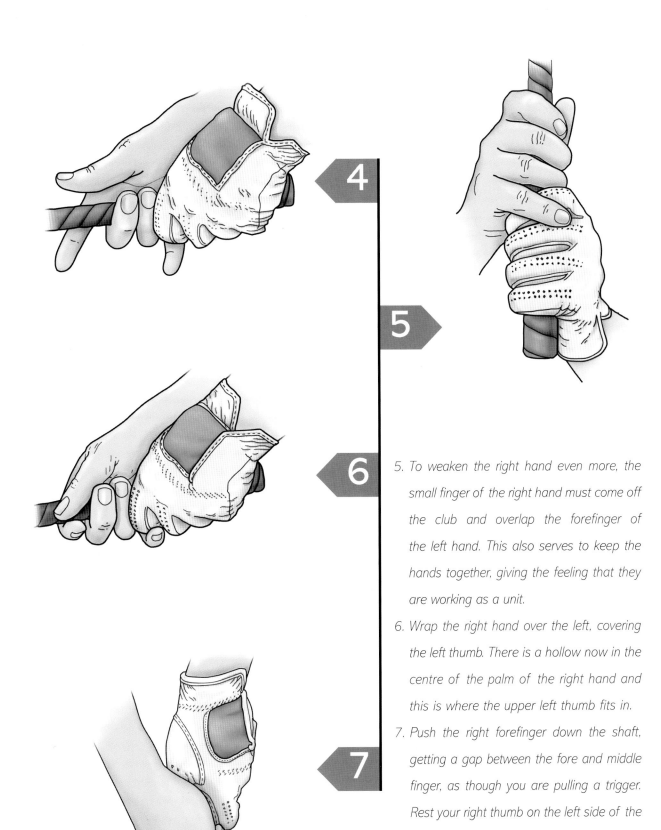

4

5

6

7

5. To weaken the right hand even more, the small finger of the right hand must come off the club and overlap the forefinger of the left hand. This also serves to keep the hands together, giving the feeling that they are working as a unit.

6. Wrap the right hand over the left, covering the left thumb. There is a hollow now in the centre of the palm of the right hand and this is where the upper left thumb fits in.

7. Push the right forefinger down the shaft, getting a gap between the fore and middle finger, as though you are pulling a trigger. Rest your right thumb on the left side of the club, not on top. Put no pressure on your left thumb with your right hand. Your right hand should be weak.

Posture

Your weight should be evenly distributed on the soles and heels of both your feet. Your legs must be ever so slightly flexed, not rigid and not overly bent. To get your spine in the correct position, stand upright and hold the club in front of you with the left arm straight and your elbows touching your sides.

Now bend forward from the hips, with the feeling that your backside is sticking out slightly. Do not bend from the waist. Your lower back must be straight to enable your torso to rotate in the swing.

Your heels should be about 1ft (30cm) apart. It should be easy for you to transfer your weight from one foot to the other. Your right foot should be square to the target line. This serves to restrict the right knee on the backswing, ensuring you don't sway (*see* p100). Turn your left foot out to the left by about 30 degrees. This will make it easier for you to turn your hips on the downswing and to follow through. Lean the shaft of the club ever so slightly to the left with your hands in line with the ball and your left ear. At no stage during the swing should your head be in front of the ball.

Different stances

Your set-up position will influence the path of the clubhead. Ideally you should set up with the club pointing directly at the target and the feet parallel to that line. A poor set-up position will invariably lead to a poor shot. Take great care with this.

Square stance

Your feet and shoulders are parallel to the target line. From this position you will swing the club downwards and through directly towards the target.

Closed stance

Your body is aligned to the right of the target, enabling you to swing the club down inside the target line and to put right-to-left spin on the ball.

Open stance

Your body is aligned to the left of the target which makes it easy for you to swing the club downwards from outside the target line and to put left-to-right spin on the ball.

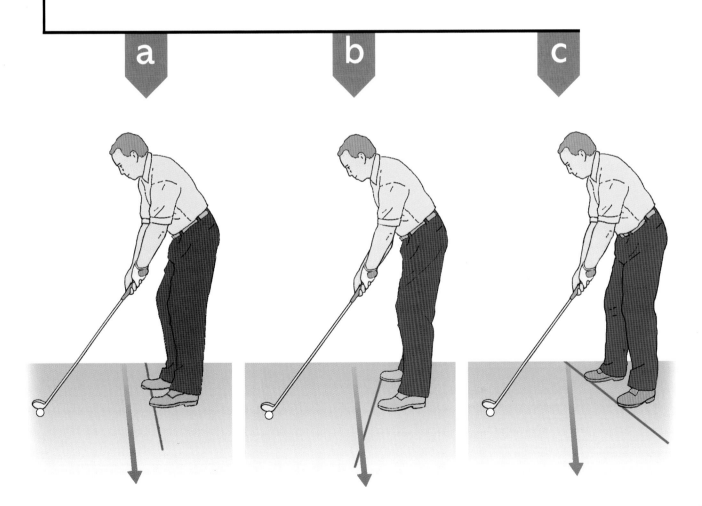

a b c

Working the ball

It is possible to put any spin on a golf ball. If you want it to move right-to-left you have to hit the right half of the ball from inside the target line with the clubface pointing left. If you want the ball to move left-to-right, you must hit the left half of the ball from outside the target line with the clubface pointing slightly to the right.

If you need the ball to fly lower, position it further back in the set-up. This reduces the loft of the club-face, from say that of a seven-iron to that of a six-iron, but because the seven-iron has a shorter shaft, the ball won't fly as far as if it were hit with a six-iron. If you need the ball to fly higher, place it further left in the set-up. This increases the loft of the club, but reduces the distance of the ball, which is ideal for 'inbetween' shots for a particular club where the distance to the flag is not spot-on. Simply holding the club a bit lower down on the shaft will also enable you to hit the ball a few yards shorter than normal. All of these shots need to be tried out on the practice tee.

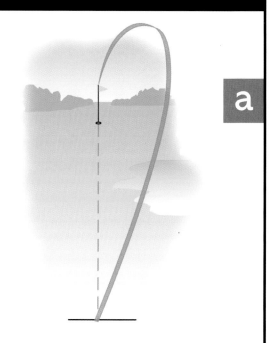

⬆ *If you can hit the ball past the water hazard, then rather set up to the right of it and draw the ball around it (see opposite).*

a

⬇ *When aiming away from the water hazard ensure you have sufficient loft on your club to get your ball over it. Dropped shots can be very costly.*

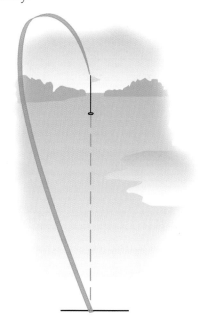

b

Putting spin on the ball

a

To impart left-to-right spin the clubhead must approach the ball from outside the target line and the clubface must be pointing to the right as in the fade (see opposite). The grip should be altered to show only one knuckle on the back of the left hand, preventing the club from closing in the hitting zone

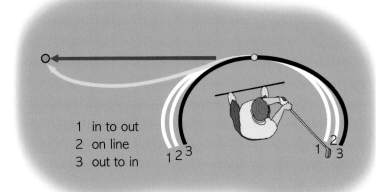

1 in to out
2 on line
3 out to in

b

To impart right-to-left spin the clubhead must approach the ball from inside the target line and the clubface must be pointing to the left as in the draw (see opposite). There should be three knuckles visible on the back of the left hand, enabling the hands to rotate anticlockwise in the hitting zone.

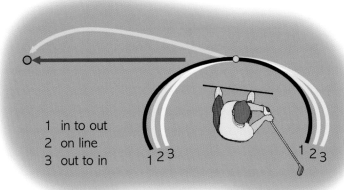

1 in to out
2 on line
3 out to in

Lofting the ball

When you stand over the ball, you must know that you have the right club in your hands. The slightest hesitation can create tension during a swing, altering your tempo and ruining the shot.

You must know exactly how far you will hit each ball. An average golfer should hit a ball about 150yds (137m) with an eight-iron. (This varies depending on build and ability.) Between clubs there is a difference of 10 to 15yds (9 to14m).

To ascertain the distance you are hitting your balls get to the practice area and hit 20 balls with a nine, seven and five-iron. Pace out the distance to the centre of where each group of balls has landed to work out the average distance for each club. Make a note of how far you hit the ball and what distance you are from the flag.

The wind will affect the flight of your ball. Allow for this. A slight breeze blowing into you does not mean you should hit harder, rather use a longer club and not the usual club for that distance. The landing area will also affect your club choice and if the green is hard you may need to drop the ball short. Even the way you are feeling on a particular day could affect your club selection: you might be playing well, feeling aggressive and hitting the ball a few yards further than if you were feeling otherwise. So you should allow for this.

Wedges

Use wedges within 110yds (100m) of the green. Because of the loft on these clubs golfers are able to hit the ball relatively high and impart a lot of backspin. These clubs are used for a variety of shots including chipping, pitching, bunker and full shots.

lob-wedge 56 loft
sand-wedge 52 loft
pitching-wedge 50 loft

lob-wedge/77yds (70m)
sand-wedge/87yds (80m)
pitching-wedge/98yds (90m)

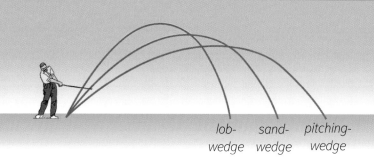

*lob-
wedge*   *sand-
wedge*   *pitching-
wedge*

Irons

By using different irons you will be able to hit the ball at different distances. The height the ball flies and the distance it travels depends on the loft or angle of the clubface and the length of the shaft. The distances will obviously vary slightly from person to person and those shown here are merely a guide.

9 iron/130yds (119m)
8 iron/140yds (128m)
7 iron/150yds (137m)
6 iron/160yds (146m)
5 iron/170yds (155m)
4 iron/180yds (164m)
3 iron/190yds (174m)
2 iron/200yds (183m)

9 8 7 6 5 4 3 2

Woods

The woods have longer shafts than the irons and hit the ball further. There is a wide range of metal woods designed to suit different people with different swing styles. Some golfers replace their long irons, such as 3-, 4- and 5-irons, with woods such as 5-, 4- and 3-woods. The woods hit the same distances as the irons, but the golfers find them easier to use. You are permitted to carry any combination of clubs.

5-wood/21 loft
3-wood/15 loft
driver/10 loft

5-wood/219yds (200m)
3-wood/246yds (225m)
driver/273yds (250m)

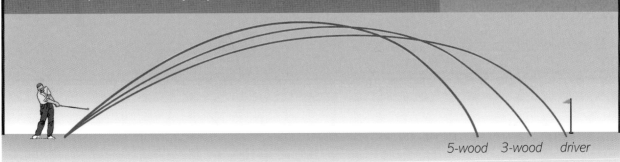

5-wood   3-wood   driver

The Swing

A golf swing is a coordinated movement involving the hands, arms and torso. The torso is the axle of the swing which directly affects the movement of the arms. The faster you turn your torso, the faster your arms will rotate. Your hands form the last link in the sequence of the swing providing extra clubhead speed in the hitting area. The effectiveness of your swing depends largely on the position of your hands and the flexibility of your wrists, and as a result, you will need to devote a lot of attention to your grip.

The backswing

Relaxing during the backswing is hard. If your muscles tense up, especially those of your right arm and shoulder, you will not be able to take the club back smoothly. Your torso must move in unison with your upper arms which, in turn, gently touch your sides. The backswing must be a single movement, with every body part moving except the right knee.

Your main focus must be on turning your shoulders until your back is facing the target, and to swing the club back slightly inside the target line. Your hips should turn as you turn your upper body, and they should not do so more than 45 degrees, or half as much as the shoulders. Keep the arc of the club as wide as possible and feel that your hands are stretched away from your chest. The wider the arc, the more clubhead speed you will be able to generate later in the swing.

1

Keep your right shoulder over the outside of your right knee. Keep the lower half of your body solid and your knees slightly bent in order to build resistance in your swing.

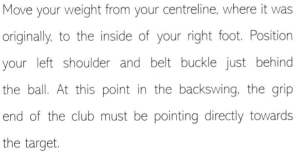

Move your weight from your centreline, where it was originally, to the inside of your right foot. Position your left shoulder and belt buckle just behind the ball. At this point in the backswing, the grip end of the club must be pointing directly towards the target.

Take the pressure off your left foot and get your left knee roughly in line with the ball without raising your left heel off the ground by more than an inch. At the top of the backswing your hands should be as high as the top of your head (with the left hand still firmly on the club) as well as behind it, in line with your right shoulder. The club should be on line pointing at the target or just above it. Don't consciously break your wrists. If your right wrist is relaxed, this cocking action will occur on its own, giving you an angle of about 90 degrees between your left forearm and the club.

The downswing

The start of the downswing determines the quality of a shot. (This is when all players tend to tighten their right hands and hit much harder and sooner than is required.) Keeping your right side under control during it is possibly the most important factor in the game.

Your first objective must be to move your hips until your belt buckle is just ahead of the ball. You need to achieve this without straightening your right hand and arm so as to generate clubhead speed.

If you straighten your right arm too early in the downswing, the club will strike the ground before it gets to the ball and you will hit what is known as a fat shot (see p94). Also, if there is too much tension in your right side at the start of the downswing, your right shoulder will not move under your chin as it is meant to, but rather around it. This will cause the club to be too high when it reaches the ball and you will hit what is termed a thin shot (see p95).

1

Push your knees slightly towards the left, transferring weight to your left foot. Advance your left hand and hip in a single movement. Start to rotate your hips anticlockwise along with your knees. This will cause your torso to rotate, which will pull your arms down and they, in turn, will pull your club down. Aim to get your belt buckle pointing at least 45-degrees left and ahead of the ball, or almost halfway to the target.

2

3

Begin to swing your hands downwards towards the ball, but keep them inside the swing plane. Move your right elbow downwards towards your right hip and tuck your right arm into your side. If you keep your right hand relaxed, you will find that the clubhead will tend to drop down behind you, staying inside the swing plane. Once your hands are at hip height move your left hip away from the ball and get the right hip pocket past it.

Straighten your right arm and then your left leg. Transfer your weight onto your left heel. Using your right hand and arm accelerate the club through the ball, getting the clubhead to reach top speed in the direction of the target. Keep your head in place just behind the ball. By the time the club gets to the ball, your chest should be facing left of it.

The follow-through and finish

A good follow-through results from a good downswing; the club swings through directly towards the target due to a late release of the hands.

Your left arm should be rotating anticlockwise, with your right hand rolling over your left, picking up clubhead speed and squaring the clubface at the same time. Your left arm must remain straight, all the way through the hitting area, keeping the clubhead on line. Turn your torso and chest towards the target to keep your left arm straight. Follow the club.

With most good golfers, their right arms straighten just after impact, as they use their right hands to drive the clubs through. Some really good players are able to keep their right arms bent all the way through to the finish.

You must develop a feeling of staying down, with your torso still angled in the same position as it was at address. You do not have to stand upright to watch the flight of the ball; turn your head without pulling the torso out of position. At impact, and all the way to the finish keep your right shoulder lower

1

Just after impact, position the body in such a way that your left leg is straight, your weight is on your left heel and your belt buckle is just ahead of the ball. Keep your head behind the ball and your right shoulder under your chin.

than your left. Balance is important through the swing. If you cannot maintain your balance at the finish, it is either because you are swinging too hard and fast, your head has moved out of position or your left leg is bent. Most of your weight should be on your left foot at the finish, with minimal weight on the toes of your right foot.

Just as you need to control your movements in other parts of the swing, so too do you need to do so here. The later you use your right hand in the downswing, the longer your follow-through will be. If you hit too early in the downswing, your follow-through will be short and incomplete.

Swing the club through towards the target, keeping your left arm straight all the way until about hip height. At this stage you can bend your arms and swing the club upwards and over your left shoulder. Getting a picture-perfect finish will help you maintain your tempo and balance.

2

Your left hip now becomes the pivot point of the swing. Turn your chest towards the target, allow your right shoulder to get past the ball and to continue swinging towards the target. When your right knee and hip get past the point where the ball was, swing the club all the way through until it is behind your head. Your left forearm should be pointing to the sky at the finish, your left hand still firmly on the club and your club should be more or less horizontal to the ground.

chapter 3

The Short Game

Putting on the green, chipping from the grass around the green and playing shots from the bunkers next to the green are collectively known as the short game. Getting the ball onto the green in the required number of shots is what we term 'hitting the greens in regulation'. If you study the statistics, you will see that even the world's best golfers very seldom hit all the greens in regulation. They usually miss an average of about five greens per round. They are still able to make very good scores, however, most often under par, only because of their ability to chip and putt well.

To make a reasonable score you need a reasonable short game. Very few people work on improving their chipping and putting, yet these are the areas where a little practice would bring a huge improvement to their score. If you can't get to the practice green, chip on your lawn at home or putt on the carpet.

With the short game, confidence plays a big part. Knowing that chipping and bunker shots hold no fear for you, will allow you to relax a bit on your iron shots to the green and take some pressure off your long game.

➲ *Chipping calls for a wide range of shots, each adapted to suit a particular situation. Practice and experience will help you decide which clubs to use for the various shots.*

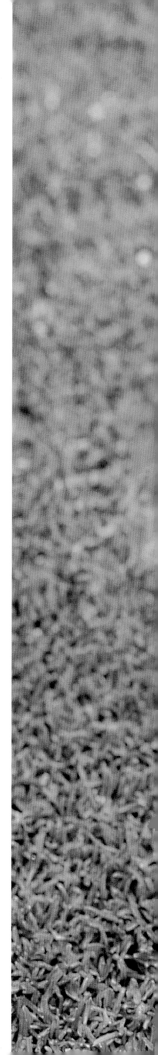

Chipping

Chipping comprises playing short shots from the edge of the green – up to about 30yds (30m) around it. You can use any club to chip, but the lob-wedge, sand-iron and pitching-wedge are often used. The better your choice of club, the better your chances of getting the ball near the hole.

Before you decide which club to use ask yourself: What sort of lie does the ball have? How close to the edge of the green must the ball land? How far does the ball need to run? Is it on an uphill or downhill slope and, most importantly, with which type of shot am I most confident? When playing a standard shot, use a pitching wedge. Get the ball to land about a yard (1m) from the edge of the green and allow it to roll up to the hole. If the ball is close to the green use a nine-iron to get the ball on the green earlier and allow for more run. If the ball is further from the green use a sand-iron or lob-wedge to allow for a larger margin of error and less run. When playing over a bunker always

🎧 *When preparing to hit a chip shot, visualize where on the putting surface the ball is going to land and what club you're going to choose to achieve this.*

use a lob-wedge or sand-iron to get the ball in the air and over the bunker. From the edge of the green you can even use a putter or, if the grass is not smooth enough, a seven or eight-iron to run the ball along the green. Remember to hit the ball on the downswing and not the upswing and do not hit it hard to get it to fly further.

Regardless of the chipping shot you're playing, set up square with your feet on line to the target. Flex your knees slightly and angle them to the left, with most of your weight on your left foot. Keep your hands and belt buckle just ahead of the ball so that you are able to hit down on the ball. Position the ball in the centre of your feet. Keep your hands close to your body (your upper arms should touch your sides). During the back-swing keep your head, knees and hips steady, your wrists flexible and the clubhead lifted slightly. In the downswing, turn your upper body, chest, arms and club down and through towards the target. If your chest does not turn, your left arm will collapse and your club will swing through to the left. Your follow-through must be solid. Get the feeling that your left arm and club are in a straight line at the finish. Keep your wrists firm, the clubface square to the target and swing the club through on the correct line.

Chipping options

In order to get the ball close to the hole, you will need to adapt to the situation at hand. The more green you have between the ball and the hole, the less loft you need. Using an eight-nine or nine-iron such as in illustration A, allows for a short swing, but causes the ball to roll further. A more lofted club such as a sand-wedge or lob-wedge, requires a long swing, but gets the ball to fly high and stop quickly such as in illustrations B and C.

Clubface angles

The clubface must point at your target as in illustration C, enabling you to get your hands slightly ahead of the ball. An open clubface, such as in illustration A, is when the clubface points to the right of the target. A closed clubface, such as in illustration B, is when the clubface points to the left of the target.

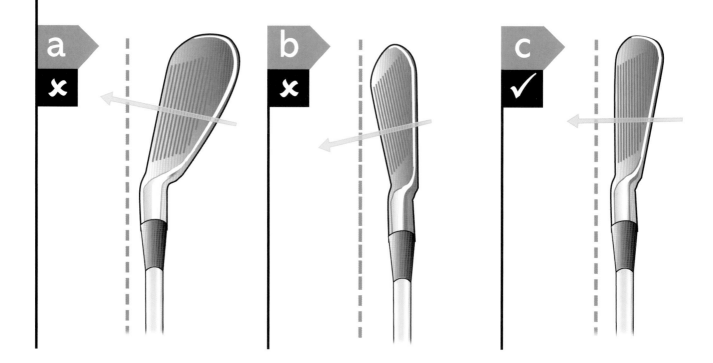

Bunker shots

A bunker is a hazard filled with sand and fills most golfers with trepidation. With a little practice using the right technique, you will soon discover that it is actually the easiest shot in the game.

With a bunker shot the club does not touch the ball at all, instead the club slides under it and the sand pops it into the air.

Hitting a ball off grass requires a great deal of accuracy in order to avoid a thin or fat shot (*see* p94). With a short bunker shot, you don't need that sort of precision – with a bunker shot of 10 or 15yds (9 or 13.7m) you could hit about 2in (5cm) behind the ball and still get it on the green. You could also hit 3in (8cm) or even 4in (10cm) behind the ball and it would still pop out of the bunker.

When hitting a bunker shot, remember to stand fairly 'open' at address with your feet pointing left of the target. 'Flatten' the club a bit to allow for more loft. The more you 'flatten' the clubface, the more it will point to the right, and you will need to align your

feet further left to compensate for this. Aim to hit the sand about 2in (5cm) behind the ball.

The backswing with this shot is slightly different in that you need to break your wrists a lot earlier and get the club pointing to the sky with the shaft vertical. Your left arm should be just about horizontal to the ground, if not a bit more. It is better to get the backswing too long than too short.

The biggest mistake most players make with a bunker shot is that they stop at the ball, with little or no follow-through. Because the backswing is relatively long for such a short shot, their instinctive reaction is to stop it, for fear of the ball hurtling over the green. If you stay down and allow the club to slide under the ball, it will not fly far at all.

Keeping your head steady when playing a bunker shot is very important. Get the club under the ball and follow through towards the target.

Softer sand will require that you swing longer as the club slides through deeper and quicker in soft sand than in hard sand and you need to compensate for this. If the sand is hard, keep your wrists firmer and work on getting under the ball, ensuring the club does not bounce off the sand and hit the ball on the upswing.

Bunker shots

Dig your feet into the sand to build a firm base, with your legs flexed and your knees angled to the left. Get your weight just left of your centreline. Hold your club a bit lower than normal with the same grip as other shots. Keep your wrists fairly flexible.

Turn your shoulders, but keep your legs and hips pretty much where they started. Focus on keeping your head absolutely steady and your torso bent over the ball.

Move your left hip forward, pull it out of the way and keep your weight on your left foot. You must turn your chest towards the target, and drag your arms behind.

Turn your torso so you end up facing the flag. Keep your grip pressure fairly firm to allow for a solid follow-through. Keep the clubface open on this shot. Do not roll your right hand over your left as with a normal swing.

Pitching

A shot of roughly 30yds to 90yds (27 to 82m) is termed a pitch. This shot is longer than a chip, but shorter than a full swing (the length of the swing will vary according to the distance from the flag).

You can play pitch shots with any wedge, depending on the type of shot required. The action is slightly different to the full swing as you want to avoid excessive hip movement on your backswing. Keep the lower half of your body firm and your legs steady. 'Break' your wrists earlier than you would with a full shot and keep your left arm roughly horizontal to the ground at the top of the backswing.

Start the downswing by moving your legs and hips to the left. Your arms and hands can then swing through straight towards the target. Turn your chest towards the flag on the downswing and lag your arms behind. Keep your wrists fairly firm and follow through to the flag. Never help the ball into the air. Hit it slightly on the downswing and stay down as you swing through.

Your club selection will depend on circumstances: If the flag is at the back of a long green, you might use a wedge or even a nine-iron and allow for some run. If the flag is close to the front edge of the green you will need a sand-iron or lob-wedge to stop the ball sooner.

These shots are usually to save par on par-fours and to set up birdie chances on par-fives. Missing the green with a pitch is always annoying and will probably lead to more bad shots, so practise these shots as often as you can.

A pitch shot is basically a half swing with all the body movements reduced accordingly. Position the ball in the centre of your feet with your hands and belt buckle slightly ahead of the ball.

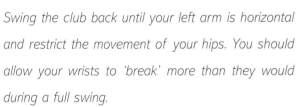

2

Swing the club back until your left arm is horizontal and restrict the movement of your hips. You should allow your wrists to 'break' more than they would during a full swing.

3

Keep your head very steady and turn your chest towards the flag as you follow through. Hit the ball on the downswing and complete the movement with your weight on your left foot.

Putting

Most golfers think of putting as a separate game altogether; good putters make it look so easy, but for most of us it is usually very difficult.

Here's how to putt well: keep your eyes directly over the ball and your putter low to the ground during a swing. Always keep your strokes slow and smooth, your putter on line to the hole and the clubface pointed directly at the target all the way through.

Keep your entire right hand on the club in order to 'feel' with it; and stretch your left forefinger down over the fingers of your right hand. This will keep your hands working together, preventing your left wrist from collapsing and maintaining your swing on line.

The exact positioning of your hands is a personal choice. Experiment as much as possible, trying different putters, hand positions and set-ups. Alter your grip pressure to see how it affects your 'feel' and stroke. (Few good putters use only their hands).

With putting, the swing is usually a pendulum action, with hands, arms and shoulders working together. For the tempo and the action think of a grandfather clock: 'Tick-tock. Tick-tock.' Simple, but it works.

There are no strict rules regarding putting. Basically, if it works for you, it's fine. Good putters have about 25 and 30 putts per round, with average putters having about 33. If you have more than 33 putts per round, your technique needs some urgent attention.

1

Get your feet on line to your target and touch your sides with your upper arms. Keep your hands as 'soft' as possible to get as much 'feel' as you can.

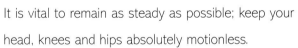
2

3

It is vital to remain as steady as possible; keep your head, knees and hips absolutely motionless.

Keep your follow-through longer than your backswing. Stroke the ball rather than hit it.

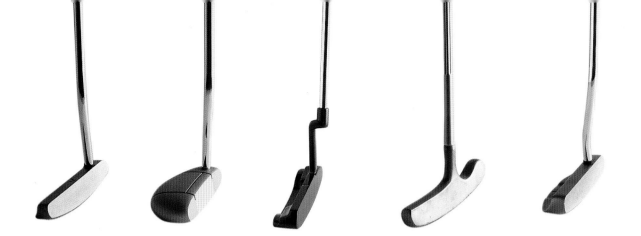

Putters

No two golfers address the ball in the same manner. Some feel comfortable with their legs fairly straight, while others putt with their legs bent. There are those who have their arms straight when they putt and others who keep their arms tucked into their sides. Tall people bend over the ball more and some position the ball closer to their feet than others.

Because of this variation in individual postures, a wide range of putters has developed over the years. In the early to mid-1900s the blade putter was generally the only model available, and a lot of golfers managed to putt extremely well with them.

The centre-shafted putter came onto the market, and that was followed by the heel and toe putter. The concept of heel and toe weighting has been extended to every club in the set and is now the major factor in golf technology.

The basic principle behind heel and toe weighting is that if you do not strike the ball in the centre of the clubface, the design of the club will keep the club pointing towards the target. Alignment is obviously an important factor, and this also forms a major part of modern putter design. The shape and size of putters

There are a wide variety of putters. Most golfers will try a number of them during their lifetimes, but generally, a person with a good putting action will not be limited in what they can do with any one of them. Long-handled putters and belly putters are certainly worth trying – the top end of their shafts anchor your body and eliminate any unnecessary movement. Pictured here from left to right are the blade putter, mallet putter, offset heel-toe putter, famous 'bull's eye' style putter and a putter with a milled face.

has changed dramatically over the years, with modern putters incorporating sophisticated hi-tech features.

To cater for individual preferences, putters are available with varying lie angles, weights, grips and even different lofts. When choosing a putter, find one that allows the sole of the club to rest flat on the ground when you are in the address position. You must also feel comfortable with the weight of the club, the length of the shaft and the size of the grip.

Putting grip

How you position your hands on the club while putting is up to you. Experiment as much as possible until you find a grip that suits you. A small alteration to it could make a huge difference to your score. Here are two examples with which to start: the reverse overlap and the 'Langer' grip.

The reverse overlap is the most common putting grip used by professionals the world over. To form it, first keep the palms of your hands facing each other.

Place your hands in the centre of the rubber grip to optimize the balance of the putter. Position your thumbs on top of the shaft and your left forefinger over the little finger of your right hand.

The 'Langer' grip

The 'Langer' grip is named after the famous German golfer who used it to eliminate the yips (see p98). The Langer grip locks the left forearm in place so that the wrists are not involved in the stroke at all.

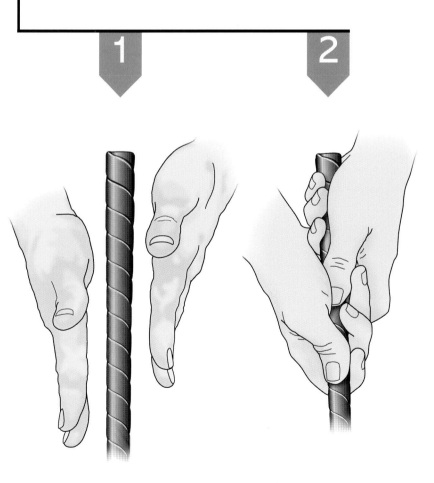

1

2

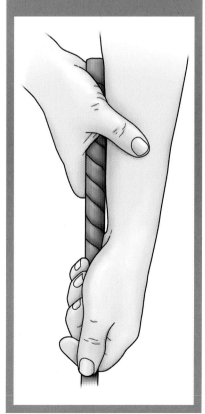

Reading the green

To determine the line and weight of the putt, you have to study the green: look at the slopes, the length and grain of the grass, as well as its dampness and dryness and, in extreme cases, even take the wind into account.

The general slope of the green is noticeable even to a beginner. The more you play and practise on undulating greens, the better you will become at judging the line and weight of the putt. Your target line obviously depends on the slope you're playing. On all except the very shortest putts, you almost certainly have to allow for some 'break' or turn. Any ball, on any uneven surface, will roll to the lowest point and you have to judge how much that turn will be.

While approaching the green you should make a mental note of its overall slope. Once you get to your ball, study the grass between your ball and the hole more closely. Most modern courses have bent grass on their greens – a fine, usually grain-free type.

Some courses have coarse grass where its grain is visible and effects the way you play a ball. Its grain lies flat – usually in the direction of the nearest source of water – and this always causes the ball to turn in this direction.

The first green you play will give an indication of what the others will be like. Make a note of whether they have been cut or watered that day. When the green is really soft as a result, it means you can expect less run with your approach shots.

It is also worth examining the holes (the low side of the hole is usually more worn than the other). Aim for the side that is not worn.

📖 *Take note of the slope of the green and factor this in when choosing a line to putt.*

Plumb bobbing

Plumb bobbing requires a bit of practice before trying it out on the course. Part of mastering the technique is determining, which one of your eyes is dominant, because that is the eye you will require to judge your target line. Hold your putter about midshaft. Extend your arm with your club straight up. Focus on the flag ahead of you and then close one eye. If the flag moves then your closed eye is dominant.

❶*Get down on your haunches and position your eyes close to the ground. In this way, you will get a very clear indication of the undulations on your target line.*

❶*Place your ball just ahead of you. Hold your arm out, with your hand about midshaft and the club shaft vertical. Your ball should take the path of the line between your club and the hole.*

chapter 4

Tempo, Timing and other Essentials

Preparation, both off and on the course, is always important when trying to improve your long game. It gives you an edge over your competitors and fills you with confidence.

Regular practice will improve your fitness and enable you to play more efficiently. The type of clubs you choose to buy will also determine the quality of your shots as will the peace of mind afforded by effective time management prior to a game.

On the golf course, strategy is essential in the build-up to a swing. If there is trouble down the right side of the fairway, for example, visualize working the ball away from it. If the fairway is really narrow, you might need to prepare to swing a bit easier. Knowing how to select an appropriate club, according to the distance a ball needs to travel and how the swing plane and club lie work, will serve you well in this regard – all information provided in this chapter. It also includes guidelines on how to improve your aim, balance, tempo and timing.

➲ *There is no such thing as a natural game of golf. Every golfer has to hit thousands of balls to develop a good swing.*

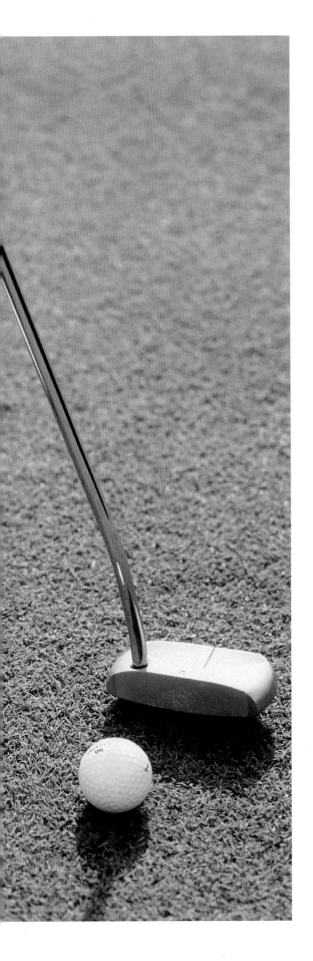

Off-course management
Practice

To practice with a purpose is the only way to achieve a good game. Try to practise every day. Aim at playing 100 full shots, 200 chips and 300 putts. To keep your swing good you need to hit about 200 balls a day. If you can't get to the practice area, chip on the lawn at home, putt on the carpet or simply swing a club with your left hand.

When trying to perfect your swing work on one part of the sequence at a time, and as you perfect each movement, move on to the next. This may take days, even weeks, and requires willpower.

Get a friend to take photographs or a video of your swing and compare your techniques with that of good golfers. Few of us really know what we look like during our swing and these images may help tremendously. You can also get someone to watch you and tell you if you are getting it right.

Never practise downwind or with the wind blowing in a left-to-right direction. If you do, you will end up swinging across your projected swingpath in an effort to get the ball to the flag.

☞ *If you are expecting to see any improvement in your performance, it is recommended that your daily practice regimen include 200 chips and 300 putts.*

Time management

It is extremely important to get to the course in good time. Top golfers get to the course about 90 minutes before their tee-off times, and you should allow for a similar amount of time to prepare for your round.

Build up your confidence by hitting 30 to 40 shots before your round, starting with a wedge, then with a seven and four-iron, and a driver. After that, practise your chipping and putting, working on developing a slow rhythmical action.

Apart from allowing you to warm up for your game and redirecting your focus, the time before you tee off also allows you to acclimatize to the environment and rid yourself of any work-related stress.

When you start your game, the speed of play can also vary. Walk at a pace that will enable you to maintain your position on the course, not holding up those behind nor causing you to wait for those ahead.

On average, most golf courses are about 7500yds (6800m) in length. Getting from one green to the next tee adds to this distance, as does the fact that one does not walk in a straight line on the course. You could walk a total of 7 miles (10km) during a round, and if you are not particularly fit, you will need to factor this in as well. Pace yourself carefully, especially on undulating courses where you may encounter long, uphill stretches to the holes. On the last few holes you might be tired and this could affect the quality of your shots. Most people start forcing in this situation, and you might have to use a longer club than you normally would.

Carrying your own bag or pulling a cart is more strenuous and will exacerbate matters. Nowadays, riding in a buggy is fairly common and, in fact, there are courses where buggies are compulsory. They certainly ease the physical demands of the game, especially for the elderly. The one drawback with buggies, though, is that you will have longer periods to wait if the people ahead of you are walking, and this could affect your concentration.

Carrying your own golf equipment on the golf course can be strenuous, so getting a caddy to help you in this respect can greatly increase your enjoyment of the game.

Buggies are useful on a golf course and minimize the duration of a game where time is of the essence.

Equipment

There are many golf clubs available to suit a wide range of tastes. Try out as many putters as you can. Select one that feels comfortable in your hands and that swings on line easily. Most importantly, you must actually like the look of it.

Beginners have access to a wide selection of good starter club sets that they can purchase new or used. A good quality used set could in actual fact last them longer than a new entry-level starter set, and may be a better bet. Ladies and senior golfers should go for graphite shafts. The overall weight of these clubs is lighter than those with a steel shaft and they are easier to swing. The shaft flex should be regular or ladies. Stiff shafts should only be used by really strong golfers who swing clubs through very quickly.

Lower-handicap golfers usually have a very good idea of what club they want. The shafts, heads and the grips all have different appearances and feel.

Overall, all clubs might do exactly the same job, but you must feel comfortable with your choice. Visit a local golf shop and find a pro who can help you decide.

➲ *Try as many clubs as possible before deciding on what to buy. Modern computer equipment can show which shaft flex will suit you best.*

Club selection

You are allowed to carry a maximum of 14 clubs when you play golf. You can choose which clubs you would like to have with you. If you are more confident with woods, then add more woods. If you want two putters, then take two putters. Put together a set of clubs with which you feel most comfortable; they don't have to all be the same brand.

The short irons – from the eight-irons down to the wedges – are not a problem. These clubs have a loft of between 100 and 150yds (90 and 137m). The middle-irons (the five, six and seven-irons) sometimes stray off the target line and the long irons (the two, three and four-irons) are usually a nightmare.

Many people feel more comfortable with woods than long-irons – never feel that you are incapable if you struggle with the long-irons. If you feel more confident with woods then use them. There are those that match the distance of long irons, and they usually get the ball to fly a bit higher. The driver is the longest club and gets the ball to fly the furthest. If you struggle with the driver then use a three-wood until your swing improves.

It is difficult to ignore peer pressure, but play your own game with the equipment that works for you. Try different brands as often as you can, and you will soon develop a feel as to what suits you and what doesn't.

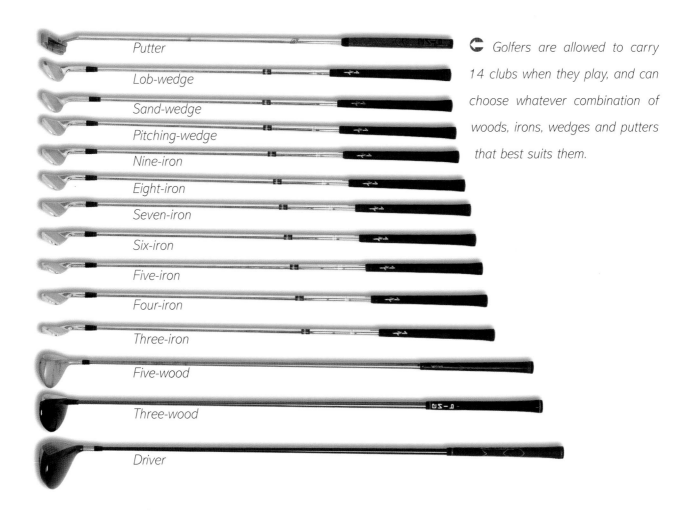

Putter

Lob-wedge

Sand-wedge

Pitching-wedge

Nine-iron

Eight-iron

Seven-iron

Six-iron

Five-iron

Four-iron

Three-iron

Five-wood

Three-wood

Driver

☾ *Golfers are allowed to carry 14 clubs when they play, and can choose whatever combination of woods, irons, wedges and putters that best suits them.*

On the course
The plane

The swing plane is the path on which the clubhead should travel during the swing. See it as a large circular disc with the bottom edge representing the position of the ball and its centre featuring your head. The clubhead should swing as close to that line as possible, but just inside it. The idea is to keep the club swinging along the line to the target and not through to the left of it. If your right side is too tense

on the backswing or the start of the downswing, you will force the club outwards through the swing plane. Work your right side under your chin on the downswing, A slight movement of the hips towards the target will get your right shoulder to drop into the correct position.

☞ *A normal swing plane with a long club tends to be 'flatter' than with a short club. Counteract this by keeping your swing more upright.*

➲ *The path the clubhead follows during the swing is called the swing plane. The ideal plane is formed by a line drawn upwards from the ball through your neck.*

Tempo

Tempo is a rather nebulous term used to describe the balance between the speed at which a golfer swings and the flight of the ball. A certain speed can feel right, but it might not be effective. In order for a swing to be effective it must be controlled – ensure the clubhead gets back to the ball in the right position, at the right time and speed.

Most golfers swing their clubs a lot faster than they need to, but when they provide the control, their clubs provide the power – a technique that takes time to perfect. When beginners start out in this game, they all instinctively grab their clubs with their right hands and hit their balls as hard as possible. This never works. Anyone starting out in this game needs a certain rhythm in the swing – a balance between energy and efficiency.

We all have a built-in natural tempo. Some people walk, talk and write fast. Others do things at a slower pace. The speed at which you swing a golf club usually fits in with this. When practising your swing speed, hit a few balls really slowly, then a few a little quicker, and then try to work out your own optimum speed and rhythm.

You need a combination of control and power, as well as the ability to put sufficient energy into the shot and to keep the club on the correct swing plane. You will soon notice that, even though individual swing speeds

may be different, good players play every single shot at an exact and consistent speed, whether they are using a nine-iron or a driver. Grip pressure in the right hand also, very often, determines swing speed and the tighter the grip, the faster the swing. It's impossible to swing a club too fast with only the left hand. Balance is the key.

Timing

A clubhead moves at different speeds during a swing. Bearing this in mind, keep your backswing relatively slow and focus on your control and balance. On the downswing, build up speed – slow at the start and then accelerate as the clubhead nears the ball. Reach top speed at the ball, continuing the momentum after the moment of impact.

At the top of the backswing there will be a 90-degree angle between your left arm and the club. To speed up the clubhead you now have to release the club. In the hitting area get the club from behind your hands to ahead of them as fast as possible. This has

to happen at precisely the right moment in order to get top speed in the right place. This is known as timing.

Golfers all instinctively hit too early, in the mistaken belief that this will produce maximum speed and maximum distance. What happens, in effect, is that their right wrist tightens up and restricts the release of the club, thus reducing the clubhead momentum. The top speed then occurs before the club gets to the ball, usually resulting in a fat shot (*see* p94), with the clubhead ploughing into the ground.

An even grip pressure and loose wrists are absolutely vital to release the club in the right place at the right time. Consciously focus on timing when you practise. Try to hit a few shots early in the downswing and a few a bit later. The term used is 'wait for it'. Wait until your hands are about hip-high before turning on the power. Get into a hitting position before you hit.

A golf swing should be relaxed, balanced and rhythmical. Any excessive tension, force or haste will always cause inconsistency in shots; most golfers tend to swing much harder and faster than they need to.

Balance

If there is a secret to the golf swing, it is balance. The two halves of your body need to work together. When the right half overpowers the left, it is impossible to get the club into the correct position. Unfortunately, a golfer's instinctive reaction is to always control the club with the stronger side.

To get the ball to take off towards the target, the club must swing through on line to it. In order to do that, your left side must pull the club through while your right side provides the power. The easiest way to achieve the correct balance, is to take your hands out of the equation and to think of your torso as the central part of your swing.

Your torso is your axle. See the wheel on a car as an analogy for the swing, with the clubhead represented by the outer edge of the tyre. The easiest way to speed up the wheel would be to spin the axle, and this is no different with the golf swing. Keep your torso directly over the ball on the downswing and turn it. The arms and hands will follow, creating a chain reaction that will result in a 'late hit', generating the clubhead speed required.

The best golf swings appear to be virtually effortless, and that is the way they are meant to be. Most golfers expend huge amounts of energy on their swings, using their hands and arms only, instead of using the larger muscles in their bodies. Think of your torso turning and pulling your arms down and through, and your hands being the last link in the sequence, whipping the club through at top speed. Once you get that, and start the downswing with your torso instead of your hands, you will see immediate results. Keep your hands completely neutral and turn towards the target.

A full follow-through and easy tempo will result in a balanced finish to the swing with the weight on your front foot.

➊ *Good balance in a shot can only be achieved if your head remains steady and you do not swing too fast.*

chapter 5

Tough Shots

Golf courses have trees, bunkers and lakes. They also have mounds, hollows, hills and valleys. All of these things are there to make the game either more interesting or more difficult, depending on your attitude, but we have to deal with them nonetheless.

Extricating the ball from awkward positions usually requires a slightly different approach; you can very seldom use the same set-up and swing you use when the ball is on a level fairway, with nicely cut grass under it, and no obstacles in the way.

No two shots in the game are ever identical. You need to evaluate each shot individually, taking all the relevant factors into account: the lie of the ball, the length of the grass, the length of the shot, the wind and, of course, your confidence level. How you are scoring at that particular stage will also affect your thinking. If you are playing well you might be more confident. If you are playing badly you might rush the shot, not really caring where it goes. The important thing is to have some idea of what the ball will do – how it will fly out of long grass or what spin it will have from a sidehill lie. You can learn these things from books, but there is nothing like personal experience.

➲ *Difficult shots are part of the game of golf and every player needs to be prepared for them. Build your confidence by practising such shots on a regular basis.*

Strategy

You never really know what to expect when you head out onto the course. So you need to prepare yourself mentally and physically for every situation imaginable, familiarize yourself with all the obstacles on the golf course and work out a strategy for any pitfalls that may befall you – this will ensure that encountering difficult shots on the course will not spoil your enjoyment of the game. (Tough shots and trick shots are explained in greater detail in this chapter and need to be practised.) Knowing how to work the ball (*see* p24), makes all the difference, as does knowing which club to use to achieve a particular loft on a ball (*see* p26).

If, for example, you need the ball to fly lower, position it further back in the set-up. This reduces the loft of the club-face, from say that of a seven-iron to a six-iron, but because the seven-iron has a shorter shaft, the ball won't fly as far as if it were hit with a six-iron. If you need the ball to fly higher, place it further left in the set-up. This increases the loft of the club, but reduces the distance of the ball, which is ideal for shots where the distance to the flag is not known. Simply holding the club a bit lower down on the shaft will also enable you to hit the ball short. All these shots need to be tried out on the practice tee.

☞ *Lakes, trees and bunkers certainly add to the beauty of a golf course, but avoid them as part of your overall game plan.*

The first-tee shot

This might just be the toughest shot in the game. Standing over the ball on the first tee is something of a nightmare. There are always people standing around the tee, waiting for their turn to play. They watch the others tee off and they know they will be watched when their turn comes. There is a steady buildup of pressure during the last few minutes of the countdown, with palms becoming sweaty and muscles tensing up. It seems strange that golfers become so tense playing a game meant to be relaxing and enjoyable.

First-tee nerves affect every one of us. Because any tension causes an increase in right-hand pressure, focus on addressing this. Try to relax every part of your body as much as possible, but keep a little pressure on the club with your left hand. Think only about tempo, playing the backswing as smoothly and slowly as possible. Keep your eyes on the ball, make a big shoulder-turn on the backswing and feel your left arm swinging the club through to the centre of the fairway. If you are affected severely by first-tee nerves use a shorter club with which you feel relatively confident, and do your best to get your ball on the fairway.

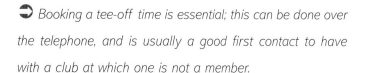

➲ Booking a tee-off time is essential; this can be done over the telephone, and is usually a good first contact to have with a club at which one is not a member.

The driver

A lot of golfers struggle with the driver. This is the longest club in the bag and it does create problems. With other clubs golfers have a fairly good idea as to how far they can hit with them. When they use the driver, however, they all instinctively try to hit the ball further than they can. They also swing faster and hit harder than with other clubs, spoiling their tempo and destroying their rhythm. The correct tempo, or the most effective swing speed, is of utmost importance here and you must maintain it with every swing you make.

The longer shaft of the club means the clubhead will be swinging through faster and there is absolutely no need to put in more effort than you do with other clubs. You must guard against excessive pressure with your right hand. Ideally, you should paint on the top of your driver the words 'seven-iron', just to remind you that you need to swing the club at the same tempo as you would a seven-iron.

The other problem is the ball position. With the driver, you need to position the ball further left than with other clubs, to ensure you hit it on the upswing, and to position your shoulders left of the target.

↺ *With the driver, position the ball further left than you would when using other clubs, and keep your shoulders directly on line to the target.*

The long irons

Long irons are more difficult to hit for only one reason: golfers think because they are holding a four-iron with a loft of 200yds (183m), that they have to hit it harder than a nine-iron that only has to fly 130yds (119m). So, they instinctively hold it tighter with their right hands, snatch it back as fast as they can and hit as hard as possible from the top. Disaster is the natural consequence.

Golf clubs have different lengths and their heads all have different lofts. A six-iron is about a half-inch (12.7mm) longer than a seven-iron with a couple of degrees less loft. This means that, if you were to execute exactly the same swing with both clubs, the head of the six-iron would travel slightly faster than that of the seven-iron, simply because its arc is slightly wider. Also, the ball would fly lower with the six-iron because the angle on its clubface is more upright than that of a seven-iron.

Maintaining the same tempo with a three-iron as with a nine-iron is the most difficult part of the game. Focus on swinging every club at exactly the same speed. Because the clubface is more upright on a long iron, any side-spin on the ball will be exacerbated. If your swing produces a fade (*see* p25) with a seven-iron, the same swing will result in a severe slice with a three-iron.

☙ *Try to maintain the same rhythm with the long irons as you do with the short irons. There is no need to swing faster.*

Tough lies

The first thing golfers do when they get to a ball is look at how it is 'lying'. We talk about 'good' and 'bad' lies, depending on what the ball is lying on, and this influences a golfer's strategy with regards to a shot.

A good lie on an average fairway requires a normal swing with a medium angle of attack. If the ball is sitting on fluffy grass and is somewhat higher off the ground, you need a shallow angle of attack, and to position the ball slightly further left in the set-up. If your club approaches the ball too steeply, it might slide under the ball, making contact too high on the clubface. This will cause the ball to pop up in the air and not go the required distance.

When the ball is lying on hard ground, with little or no grass under it, you need a steep angle of attack and to position the ball further right in the set-up. The important thing here is to ensure the club does not bounce off the ground and hit the ball thin (*see* p95). Because the ball is also positioned further back in the set-up, it will take off lower than normal and you need to put thought into your club selection.

A similar problem occurs when the ball is lying in a divot. It is more difficult to get the club back to the ball in this instance, and you need a steep angle of attack. A normal clubswing would probably get the club catching the top of the ball, hitting it thin. Play the ball back a bit in the set-up so you hit down on it. Guard against instinctively staying on your back foot and trying to scoop the ball out.

➲ *Different lies often require different strategies. Playing out of long grass or off a slope can alter the swing plane, which will affect the flight of the ball.*

Sidehill lies

No golf course is ever perfectly flat, allowing golfers a level stance with every shot. Should the ball not be on the same level as their feet the ball will react differently and they will need to make slight adjustments to their set-up.

When the ball is higher than your feet the ball will tend to fly to the left. The plane of the swing will be a bit flatter with the ball flying through to the left of the target. Use a longer club than you normally would for that distance and hold the club lower down the shaft.

Balance is important. You may instinctively pull away from the ball because you feel too close to it at address. Keep your head really steady, and relax your right side as much as possible. If your right hand exerts too much pressure you will hit a

When the ball is higher than your feet, you should hold the club down the shaft and aim slightly to the right of the target. Keep your head very steady and guard against a fat shot.

fat shot (*see* p94). The ball will also fly lower because of the flat swing. This means you will not have much backspin and the ball will run a bit further on landing.

The longer the club, the further right you need to aim. A wedge off a mild slope might fly 5yds (4.5m) to the left while a four-iron off a steep slope could fly 20yds (18m) to the left.

When the ball is below your feet, it will tend to fly to the right because of a steep angle of attack. We all tend to hit this shot from outside the target line and you must guard against hitting a shank (*see* p97). Use a longer club than you normally would and aim a bit left of the target.

◠ When the ball is lying lower than your feet bend your knees as much as possible and bend your torso over more than usual. Because the ball will tend to fly to the right of the target, allow for this when setting up.

Uphill lie

When you are playing uphill to an elevated green and your left foot is higher than the right, the ball will fly to the left of the target. Because of the slope, the ball will also fly a bit higher than normal, and not as far. To compensate for this, you need to aim right of the target and use a longer club. Again, your aim will vary, depending on the club you are using and the severity of the slope. A wedge off a mild slope will cause the ball to fly about 5yds (4.5m) left of the target, but a four-iron off a steep slope will allow the ball to fly about 20yds (18m) left. Because the ball takes off a bit higher, it might stop a bit quicker when it hits the green. This must also be taken into account when choosing the club.

☝ When playing off an upslope, the ball will tend to fly to the left of your target – allow for this. Keeping your shoulders parallel to the slope will make it easier to follow-through.

Downhill lie

Playing downhill to a green with your left foot lower than your right, is awkward. The ball will take off on a low trajectory and it won't fly as far but, because of the lower flight, it will usually run further than normal and a little right of the target.

Because of the slope you may move ahead of the ball on the downswing. In this instance, the flight of the ball will depend on what you do with your hands.

Use a shorter club and swing normally with your hands soft on the club and your head steady. Play the ball further back in the set-up to compensate for the slope and get most of your weight on your right side. This set-up and an easy swing will see the ball moving a little left-to-right. Allow for this.

⮐ When playing downhill, the ball will tend to take off on a low trajectory and you might be able to use a short club. Keep your head very steady and guard against moving ahead of the ball.

The left-handed shot

If you don't hit the ball into the centre of the fairway or the green every time, you will encounter some really tough situations. Your ball could be up against a tree or, even worse, in the tree; it could land in your opponent's golf bag or next to large rocks.

Whatever the situation, you must first know the rules. Secondly, you must be prepared to adapt to the situation. Work out your options and decide whether or not it is worth trying to play the ball as it lies. It might also be better to drop (see p122) the ball and take a penalty stroke. If you decide to play it, however, you must be fairly confident that you can get the ball into a position where you can still make a par or bogey (see p118).

One of the most common problem shots is where the ball is against a tree on the 'wrong side', and in order to hit the ball you have to play left-handed. It is worth practising this shot every now and then, just in case you get one. Use an eight-iron, and turn it on its toe. Hold the club as a left-hander would, and grip it a bit lower down the shaft.

Keep your hands and arms really rigid during the swing. Get your weight onto your front foot (now your right foot keep your hips steady and do not try to hit the ball more than 30 or 40yds (27 or 36m). This shot only makes use of your arms and shoulders, and if your hips move at all you will not make good contact. Don't try to make a full backswing or allow your wrists to get too loose. Get your hands ahead of the ball and keep them there.

1

This shot requires more control than power, so hold the club lower down the shaft than you normally would. The only objective here is to get the ball back in play.

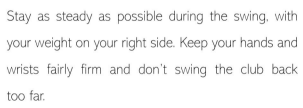

Stay as steady as possible during the swing, with your weight on your right side. Keep your hands and wrists fairly firm and don't swing the club back too far.

3

Keep your eyes focused on the ball and stay down as you follow through. Your arms and hands must remain firm throughout the swing. Guard against scooping the ball.

Playing from the Rough

The fairway is the closely cut grass between the tee and the green. The longer grass to the sides of the fairway is called the rough. The idea, of course, is not to hit your ball into the rough, but there is a very good chance that you may spend quite a lot of time in there. Once there, you should have only one thought on your mind: to get the ball out.

We all tend to underestimate the strength of long grass. A number of things happen when trying to swing a club through it. Firstly, the clubhead tends to close (*see* p38) and the longer the grass, the more it does so. This means you have to aim a little right of the target to compensate for this. Because the clubface closes, there is less loft on the club, so you need to allow for the fact that it will not fly as high as it normally does.

Secondly, the grass gets between the clubface and the ball, and the clubhead slows down as it makes contact with the grass. This means the ball does not travel as far as it would off the fairway, so make allowances for that.

With a good, clean hit off fairway grass, the club strikes the ball first and puts backspin on it. Should you get grass between the clubface and the ball, however, it will become impossible to impart back-spin. Instead, the ball will fly out of the long grass with topspin and will roll further when it hits the ground.

All of these things need to be taken into account and only experience will tell you what you can and can't do when playing out of the rough. If the ball is lying so badly that you cannot move it at all, you should consider declaring it unplayable, and dropping it in an area from where you can get it back on the fairway. Discretion usually pays.

➲ *If you stray from the fairway you can encounter some very difficult situations. Experience will eventually help you in deciding on the best course of action when trying to get a ball out of a tough spot.*

Tough bunker shots

Playing a bunker shot, is fairly straightforward when the ball is lying on smooth sand. When the sand is soft, however, the ball often becomes embedded, otherwise also known as a buried or plugged lie. When the ball is buried or you have an awkward stance, you will need to adapt your swing action to suit the circumstances. With these shots, you need to pick the club up steeper than usual in order to get the club deeper into the sand and under the ball. Usually a lob-wedge will be most effective because of its narrow sole, and the extra loft on its clubface will make it easier to get the ball out. Playing a shot from a buried lie will cause the ball to run far so it might be worth aiming away from hazards on the far side of the green.

When playing a bunker shot, it is very important to stay down during the follow-through and to ensure the club gets under the ball.

The long bunker shot

Whereas the short bunker shot is the easiest shot to play (the clubhead slides underneath the ball), the long bunker shot is the most difficult, and requires an enormous amount of practice to gain confidence with it.

With the long bunker shot, you have to take as little sand as possible, preferably none at all. The idea is to clip the ball off the top of the sand, ensuring you get the correct distance for the club. The more sand you take with the shot, the more distance you will lose. You need to keep your head absolutely steady and your left hand firm and in control; feel that it is pulling the club towards the target. Get your belt buckle ahead of the ball prior to impact to ensure you do not dig into the sand behind the ball.

Your swing must be deliberate; what you need is a full shoulder turn, with your legs fairly neutral. The downswing should involve more of your hips and shoulders, rather than your hands and arms. It is a fairly safe bet that you will hit the ball slightly fat (*see* p94) and it is usually worth taking an extra club. If the bunker has a very deep face and you need a four-iron to reach the green, but an eight-iron to clear the face of the bunker, hit the eight-iron.

◖ *To ensure the club does not dig into the sand you need to swing precisely. Maintain a light grip pressure and initiate the downswing with your hips and not your hands.*

Upslope bunker shot

This is not a particularly difficult shot, but it does require a change in strategy. Get your feet settled firmly into the sand with the ball just ahead of centre. Because of the slope it will be difficult to maintain your balance during the swing, but it is important that you remain as steady as possible.

Hitting into the upslope will cause the ball to take off a lot higher than normal and if the flag is more than 10yds (9m) from you it is often worth using a pitching wedge for this shot. If the flag is close to you, obviously a sand-wedge will do the job. Get to the practice bunker and try a few shots with different clubs, just to see which one works best for you.

Because the ball does not travel very far, you will need to swing the club back a bit further than with a normal bunker shot. This requires a lot of practice to perfect and a fair amount of courage to execute, but if you keep your head steady and get the club into the sand about 6cm (2.5in) behind the ball, you will find that it just pops into the air and does not fly far at all.

Like other awkward lies, this one is rather intimidating, but a lot easier from which to play than it originally appears to be.

☛ *Position your feet firmly in the sand with your head behind the ball. Aim about 2in (5cm) behind the ball and swing the club into the upslope. Keep your weight distributed evenly and try to maintain your balance as you swing.*

Downslope bunker shot

This is not only a difficult shot, it is often impossible. Playing from a downslope will reduce the loft of your club dramatically, and in a bunker that means you have a problem.

Most bunkers have a face to them which requires you to hit the ball out steeply in order to clear it. Because of the downslope, the ball will probably not rise at all, and if it does, it will come out on a flat trajectory and fly into the face of the bunker.

If you have a lob-wedge with more loft on it than your sand wedge, use it. Stay absolutely steady over the ball and try to get your club under it. Again, because of the slope this will prove very difficult and you may end up hitting the centre of the ball. If the bunker is very shallow and has little or no face you might get the ball out, but it may have a low trajectory and speed over the other side of the green.

Most people will obviously attempt this shot, hoping for some kind of miracle, but logic eventually forces them to rather play to the side of the bunker. Even this is difficult and should you attempt it, at least you will be able to play your next shot from the fairway.

↺ *Your backswing must be a lot steeper than with other shots. Keep your head absolutely steady during the swing. Stay low as you swing through. Your club must get under the ball.*

chapter 6

Bad Shots

A game of golf usually consists of one or two memorable shots – a few mediocre and a whole lot bad. After a round, golfers remember the good shots and are quite happy to discuss them at length. The bad shots – the slice into the water and the hook into the bush – they vow never to hit again and then play precisely these same bad shots over again in subsequent games.

The causes are invariably the same, perhaps with slightly different consequences. Whether it is the hook or the slice, the thin shot or the shank, the right hand is usually to blame. Once players understand this, they are able to get onto the practice tee and rectify their swing and, coupled with mental preparation and focus, are guaranteed an improvement in their game.

➲ *Attempting to correct habitually bad shots can at times be very frustrating, but by understanding the cause and effect of ineffective swings golfers may learn to play a better game.*

The Slice

When the ball takes off towards the target, or slightly left of it, and curves to the right, it is termed a slice.

The ball curves to the right because the club is pointing in that direction at the moment it strikes the ball, or the ball has left-to-right spin on it – or both.

A slice is also caused by right-side control during the swing. Controlling the club with the right hand will cause you to swing the club outside the target line on the back- and downswing and then through to the left of the target line. Because your right hand and wrist are quite rigid, the clubface points to the right at the moment of impact with the ball. This, combined with the outside-to-inside path of the club, imparts left-to-right spin on the ball.

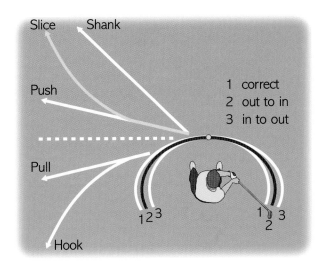

Slice   Shank

Push

Pull

Hook

1 correct
2 out to in
3 in to out

1 2 3   1 3
                2

In a slice there is right-side control during the swing. To counteract a slice, one must redress the left-to-right spin on the ball. Right-to-left spin can only be achieved by getting the club to approach the ball from inside the target line on the downswing. In order to get the club inside the target line, move the hips left at the start of the downswing. This will enable your hands to move downwards, rather than outwards, and pull the club down on the correct path. All that is required at this stage is that you keep your wrists and arms flexible enough to rotate anti-clockwise as you swing the club through towards the target. By the time the club gets back to the ball, your belt buckle must be ahead of the ball, but your head must still be behind it. Relax your right side and feel that your left side is more dominant during the swing. Your shoulders and back must form the axis of your swing, with your arms and hands playing a minor role. Concentrate on the spin you require and handle the club accordingly.

In a slice the clubface points right at impact. To counteract this, place your hands in a strong position on the club. You need to see three knuckles on the back of the left hand, and the lines formed between your thumbs and forefingers must point to the right of your chin. Swing the club down inside the target line and allow your hands to roll over in the hitting zone, getting the clubface square to the target.

The Pull

In a pull, the swing plane of the clubhead is similar to that of the slice. The clubhead also approaches the ball from outside the target line but in this instance, the clubface is pointing to the left (with the slice the clubface points to the right – the result of a different hand position at the moment of impact.)

The pull is caused by players starting the downswing with their hands rather than their hips. The hands then move outside the correct swing plane causing the clubhead to swing down towards the ball from outside the target line. Because the clubface is pointing to the left of the target line, the ball flies in a straight line, but left of the target.

In a pull, the hands start the downswing and not the hips, the shoulders are pointing left of the target and the club swings through in that direction. To correct this, start the downswing by moving your hips to the left first, enabling your hands to swing down inside the target line.

Top left: *In a pull, the right side forces the club over, getting the clubface to point left of the target line. You should relax your right side and keep your left hand firm all the way through the swing.*

Slice   Shank

Push

1 correct
2 out to in
3 in to out

Pull

1 2 3   1 3
                2

Hook

The Push

In the execution of a push, the divot is on line and the ball flies right of the target line. (Don't confuse this with a slice in which the ball curves in the air.) With a push, the ball flies in a straight line; the club is swinging through in the correct direction, but the clubface is pointing to the right of the target.

There are various reasons for this. It might be an instinctive reaction to a hook (*see* p92) wherein you tighten up your right hand and block the ball out to the right, or your hips slide into the shot with your hands too far behind the belt buckle with the clubface pointing to the right. Alternatively, you may be trying to steer the ball instead of swinging the club all the way through, swinging shorter each time in an effort to keep the ball on line.

A push results when the clubface is pointing to the right of the target. To prevent this, turn your chest towards the target as you swing through, enabling your hands to roll over in the hitting area and the clubface to square up.

To correct a push, keep your right hand soft on the club and allow it to swing through and over your left hand; some players call this 'releasing the clubhead', which squares up the clubface. Then hit through the ball, keeping your hips steady in the downswing and complete the follow-through.

The Hook

With the hook, the club approaches the ball from too far inside the target line and the clubface points left of the target at the moment of impact. This is usually caused by forcing (hitting far too hard with the right hand, resulting in the left hand collapsing in the hitting zone.)

In a hook, the clubface rolls over too much in the hitting area. To keep the clubface pointing in the correct direction, keep your left hand fairly firm on the club and relax your right hand. If your right hand becomes too strong your left hand will collapse, causing the clubface to close (see p38).

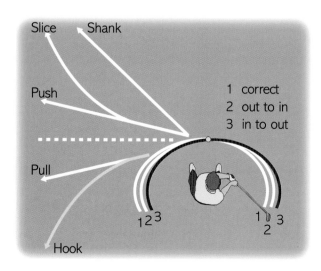

Slice   Shank

Push

1 correct
2 out to in
3 in to out

Pull

1 2 3   1   3
                 2

Hook

In a hook, the club approaches the ball from too far inside the target line. To correct this, turn your chest towards the target as you swing the club through the ball; this will enable you to keep your left arm straight in the hitting zone. Try to maintain a smooth, even tempo with all the clubs and don't use your hands in an attempt to generate power. It never works.

The Smothered Shot

This shot is very similar to the hook in that the ball flies left of the target line, but a lot lower. If your head is in front of the ball, it reduces the loft on your club, effectively causing the ball to fly low, the shoulders to point left and the club to swing through to the left of the target.

Once again, the problem is due to increased grip pressure in your right hand, and right-side domination; your right shoulder pushes towards the target and forces your head left and ahead of the ball. It may also be because you are steering the ball, shortening your backswing and tightening your wrists.

The smothered shot is the result of your head moving in front of the ball during the downswing, decreasing the loft of your club and causing it to fly too low. Remember, keep your head behind the ball during the downswing.

Top left: *To prevent the clubhead rolling over too much in the hitting area loosen your grip pressure in your right hand radically.*

The Fat Shot

In this shot, the club strikes the ground before it gets to the ball with a divot formed behind it.

There are usually only two reasons for a fat shot: either your belt buckle is behind the ball at impact or you have straightened your right arm too early in the downswing, or both. Your right hand could also be too strong on the club, forcing the clubhead downwards with excessive force.

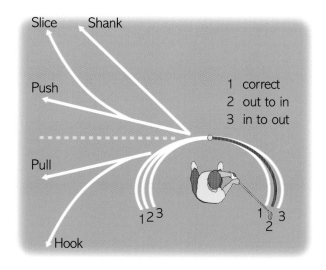

In a fat shot either your belt buckle is behind the ball at impact or you have straightened your right arm too early in the downswing, Your only thought on the downswing should be to turn your torso and keep your left hand and arm firm. This will prevent your right side from gaining control.

Top left: *In a fat shot the club hits the ground before it gets to the ball. Think about where you really need clubhead speed. This will help you release the clubhead at the right moment in the downswing.*

The Thin Shot

In this shot there is no divot and the ball flies too low. The clubface hits the centre of the ball instead of the bottom of it, also known as 'hitting it in the teeth' or 'topping the ball'. This puts topspin on the ball (a ball needs backspin to get airborne).

The most common cause of a thin shot is staying on your back foot in an effort to get the ball in the air. This results in the low point in the arc of the swing plane being behind the ball and the clubface striking it on the upswing.

Push your legs and hips to the left and transfer your weight to your left foot during the downswing. This enables you to strike with a downward blow, getting the low point in the arc of the club ahead of the ball.

Thin Shot

Do not move the hips to the left on the downswing. First rotate your hips out of the way and keep your torso flexible. Work your right shoulder downwards and keep your head at the same height all the way through.

Top left: *A thin shot results when the clubhead strikes the centre of the ball. Try to maintain the correct spine angle of the club during the swing.*

The Sky Shot

This is basically a fat shot, but because of the shape of the driver, the result is different. The driver does not dig into the ground as an iron does, but rather slides along the ground and under the ball. The top edge of the clubface strikes the ball, which flies straight into the air. It is very seldom that a sky shot is caused by the ball being teed up too high.

The basic cause of the sky shot is the same as that of a fat shot: players exert too much effort with their right hands and hit too hard and early in the downswing. On a scale of one to 10, your grip pressure should never be more than three. Rather use your torso to generate power, it's much easier.

To prevent sky shots, line up the top of the driver with the centre of the ball when teeing up (placing the ball on a peg). You can then alter the trajectory of the ball slightly by adjusting this alignment.

We all instinctively hold the driver tighter and swing it faster than we would other clubs. To counteract a shy shot, try to maintain exactly the same tempo that you would on other clubs. Hitting too early with your right hand causes a variety of bad shots. Timing with the driver is important.

The Shank

With this shot the neck of the club – where the shaft is joined to the head – strikes the ball, which takes off about 45 degrees to the right.

The reason for this is that the clubhead is further from you at impact than it would be at address. The cause, once again, is right-side dominance forcing your right shoulder outwards on the downswing, pushing the club away from you.

After hitting a shank, your instinctive reaction with the next shot may be to pull the ball to the left of the target line, making things worse. You might also 'stand up' during the backswing, getting too upright. From this position, your hands will swing outwards on the downswing, pushing the club away from you. Standing too close to the ball at address can also cause a shank.

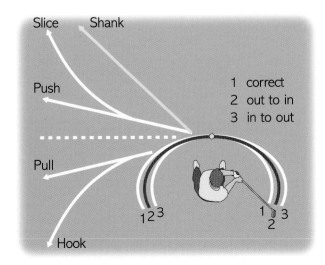

A shank is caused when the clubhead approaches the ball from the wrong direction, either from too far outside the target line, or inside it. To correct a shank, keep the club on the correct swing plane during the back and downswing.

Top left: *A shank results when the neck of a club hits the ball. Correct this by hitting the ball off the toe of the club for a while.*

The Yips

Loss of confidence can manifest in many ways and 'yipping' is one of them. The problem is purely a mental one and you need to treat is as such.

A yip is basically a shot comprising a nervous twitch of your right hand with virtually no grip pressure in your left hand. Tension and nervousness usually result in your right side becoming far too dominant, which may cause you to snatch the club back very quickly with a rigid right arm. With this shot there is no swing, tempo, timing or rhythm.

Yips are curable, but this takes time. You will need to keep your entire body rigid, especially your left hand and wrist, and then, only once you are able to hit the ball correctly, will you be able to gradually relax your right side until you have equilibrium in your hands, arms and torso, and regain a normal swing action.

Be patient and prepare yourself to work at it every single day for a few weeks. With time, you will rebuild your confidence. Practice is imperative. Keep at it.

Keep your hands, wrists and arms rigid. Hold the club a lot tighter than you normally would, and keep your hands ahead of the ball.

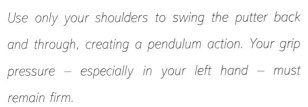

Use only your shoulders to swing the putter back and through, creating a pendulum action. Your grip pressure — especially in your left hand — must remain firm.

Keep your head steady and focus on the ball. The object of the exercise is to prevent twitching. Keep your stance solid and practise like this until you regain your confidence.

The Sway

A sway comprises moving your hips and torso from side to side, away from your centreline, when striking a ball (instead of rotating them solely around the axle point of your torso). This causes your head to move from side to side and makes it difficult for you to get your clubhead back to the ball in exactly the same position every time.

Swaying off the ball on the backswing causes the axle of your torso to get too far behind the ball, which is the cause of a fat shot. You could just as easily move too far to the left on the downswing and play a thin shot.

When practising, place umbrellas in the ground on the outsides of your feet, with the handles near your

centreline

↩In this example of a sway, the player moves his right knee out of position, causing his upper body to move away from the centreline. To prevent this, keep your right leg tense during the backswing and your torso 'over the ball'.

hips. The aim now is to swing without touching the umbrellas.

To correct a sway, you can also practise the following exercise: imagine you are standing in a drum; rotate your torso and hips clockwise and anticlockwise, but do not allow them to touch the sides of the drum. Remember, your hips must turn, not slide. The steadier your torso and hips are while doing this, the more efficient your swing will be.

To check whether your head is absolutely steady, swing a club with the sun behind you and watch your shadow.

In the follow-through to the sway, the player's head and upper body are too far to the left of the centreline. Again, to prevent this, keep your head behind the ball at all times, rotate your hips to the left on the downswing and keep your chin pointed at the ball.

centreline

chapter 7

Exercises

Each section of the swing involves different muscles which need to be trained to move in ways they have never moved before. Golfers need to build muscle memory for each of the motor skills involved in these sequences.

Do the exercises in this chapter for the shoulders, torso and hips for just a couple of minutes a day and I guarantee improvement. After just a few weeks these apparently strange movements will feel easy. Very few people exercise because they enjoy it; most of us go to gym because of the long-term benefits. View these exercises in the same way and reap the benefits.

⮊ *All sports require some degree of fitness and suppleness. Similarly, golf players need to exercise in order to build up their stamina for their games.*

The shoulders

During a golfswing the golf club will always swing parallel to the shoulders: do not point them left of the target at address or during the back and downswing. To keep the shoulders on line some people think of the right shoulder staying low, while others think of the left shoulder pulling upwards.

To get the ball to take off on line to the target, your right shoulder has to be below your chin, with your hips turned towards the target. This enables you to point your club at the ball and your belt buckle at the target during the follow-through.

The exercise described here will enable you to practise this particular movement in the swing so that it becomes more natural for you. Work at getting into the position for a few minutes everyday: initially it might be uncomfortable, but the more you practise, the easier it will become.

➲ *This exercise is designed to keep your right shoulder lower than your left as you swing the club through. Hold the golf club so that the shaft runs parallel to the shoulders (1). Simulating the downswing movement, point the grip end of the club at the ball and get your belt buckle to face the target (2).*

1

The torso

Good golfers use their torsos to swing a club, with their arms and hands playing a minor role. The torso, or upper body, is the axle of the swing, and as such, provides not only stability, but also power to generate clubhead speed.

➲ *Stand with your feet waist-width apart. Bend your arms at the elbow, so that your forearms are chest height and parallel to the ground and the backs of your hands are facing upwards. Clench your fingers lightly, knuckles almost touching. Keep your arms in this position throughout the exercise, your legs straight and hips steady. (1)*

Rotate your torso clockwise from the waist so that your back is first facing the target. (2)

Rotate your torso anticlockwise from the waist so that your chest is now facing the target. (3)

The hips

The movement of the hips is a vital component in the overall effectiveness of the golf swing in that it provides balance on the backswing and power on the downswing.

On the downswing, your hips are catalysts for the torso turn; move them slightly to the left at the start of the downswing, until your belt buckle is just ahead of the ball. Then turn towards the target, and move your weight onto your left heel. Your hips will pull your upper torso through which, in turn, will pull your arms through. Your hands are the last link in the swing sequence and create a whip-like action that gets the clubhead through at top speed.

The exercise here works to improve both the back- and downswing and is worth practising a few minutes every day. The correct movement of the hips generates enormous power through the ball without the need for force. Work at it – and enjoy the benefits.

☞ *Stand next to a chair in a standard set-up position, with your left hip about 2in (5cm) away from it. (1)*

➡ *Now simulate the follow-through of a swing. Turn your hips and torso to the left (imagine they are rotating around an axle while remaining in position), point your belt buckle in the direction of the back of the chair and put your weight onto your left foot. Do not touch the chair while doing so. (2)*

chapter 8

Etiquette
and the Rules

The game of golf originated hundreds of years ago and those who played it were called honourable gentlemen. Luckily, for most of us that term still applies. We do not have umpires watching over us, however, and we therefore need to regulate ourselves and see that we play according to the rules.

There are certain things we may and may not do on a golf course. Some of these things are learned from experience, but most are drummed into us by our teachers and playing partners. Unfortunately, there are players who bend the rules quite blatantly, which can invariably create an acrimonious situation. If possible, deal with the matter diplomatically. Explain to the person concerned that the rules apply to all of us and we all must abide by them. If he continues to disregard the rules then refuse to sign his scorecard and report his behaviour to the committee. Golf is one of the few sports where a certain decorum can still be found. Let's keep it that way.

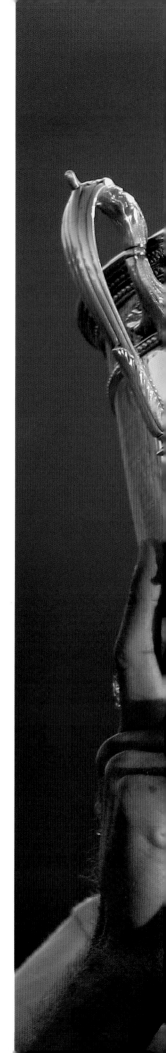

◔ *Knowing the rules and how to make them work for you assures success as it did for Retief Goosen, who turned professional in 1990. His achievements include wins at the United States Open, his first success being in 2001. Here he is seen holding the trophy after his triumph at the 2004 US Open.*

Etiquette

The Royal and Ancient Golf Club of St. Andrews is the governing body for golf worldwide. It makes, interprets and delivers decisions on the rules of golf and has published a book of rules – *Rules of Golf, 2004* – available to all golfers free of charge. This section is quoted from it.

I recommend you carry it in your golf bag and use it whenever a question pertaining to the intricacies of the game of golf arises. If in doubt, play the course as you find it and play the ball as it lies. Once back in the clubhouse, referencing your decisions to the *Rules of Golf* should help resolve any outstanding queries.

This section provides guidelines on the way golf should be played. If they are followed, all players will gain maximum enjoyment from it The overriding principle is to always consider others.

The spirit of the game

Unlike many sports, golf is played, for the most part, without the supervision of a referee or umpire. The game relies on the integrity of the individual to show consideration for other players and to abide by the rules. All players should conduct themselves in a disciplined manner, demonstrating courtesy and sportsmanship at all times, irrespective of how competitive they may be. This is the spirit of the game.

Safety

- Players should ensure that no one is standing close by or in a position to be hit by the club, the ball or any stones, pebbles, twigs or the like when they play a stroke or practice swing.
- Players should not play until the players in front are out of range.
- Players should always alert greenstaff nearby or ahead when they are about to make a stroke that might endanger them.
- If a player plays a ball in a direction where there is a danger of hitting someone, he should immediately shout a warning. The traditional word of warning in such situations is 'fore'.

Considering others

Players

Players should:

- always show consideration for other players on the course and should not disturb their play by moving, talking or making unnecessary noise.
- ensure that any electronic device they take onto the course does not distract other players.
- not tee their balls until it is their turn to play on the teeing ground.
- not stand close to, or directly behind the ball, or directly behind the hole, when a player is about to play.

On the putting green

Players should:

- not stand on another player's line on the putting green or, when they are making a stroke, cast a shadow over their line of putt.

- remain on or close to the putting green until all other players in the group have holed out.

Scoring

In stroke play, a player who is acting as a marker should, if necessary, on the way to the next tee, check the score with his team mate and record it.

Pace of play

- Play at a good pace and keep up. The Committee may establish pace-of-play guidelines that all players should follow.

- It is a group's responsibility to keep up with the group in front. If it loses a clear hole and is delaying the group behind, it should invite the group behind to play through, irrespective of the number of players in it.

- Players should be ready to play when it is their turn to. When playing on or near the putting green, they should leave their bags or carts in such a position as will enable quick movement off the green and towards the next tee. When the play of a hole has been completed, players should immediately leave the putting green.

Lost ball

- If a player believes his ball may be lost outside a water hazard or is out of bounds, he should play a provisional ball to save time.

- Players searching for a ball should signal the players in the group behind them to play through as soon as it becomes apparent that the ball will not be found easily. (They should not search for five minutes before doing so.) Having allowed the group behind to play through, they should not continue play until that group has passed and is out of range.

Priority on the course

Unless otherwise determined by the Committee, priority on the course is determined by the pace of play of a group. Any group playing a whole round is entitled to pass a group playing a shorter round.

Care of the course

Repair of damage

Before leaving a bunker, carefully fill up and smooth over all holes and footprints and any nearby that may have been made by others. If a rake is within reasonable proximity of the bunker, the rake should be used for this purpose.

Also carefully repair any divot holes made to the putting green by players, and any damage made by the impact of a ball (whether or not made by the player himself). On completion of the hole by all players in the group, you should repair any damage to the putting green caused by golf shoes.

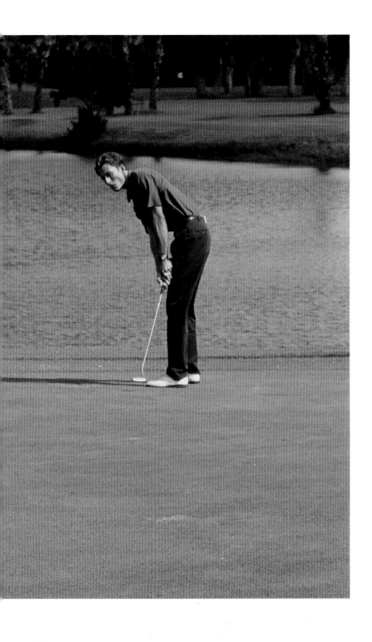

If one of your playing partners is putting from a distance you may be asked to attend the flag. This involves holding the flag until the ball is on its way, and removing it before it reaches the hole. Take care that you don't damage the hole in the process.

Preventing damage

Players should:

- avoid damage to the course by removing divots when taking practice swings or by hitting the head of a club into the ground.
- not damage the putting green by putting down their bags or flagstick on it.
- avoid damaging the hole by not standing too close it and take care when handling the flagstick and removing a ball.
- not use a clubhead to remove a ball from the hole.
- not lean on their clubs when playing on the putting green.
- Replace the flagstick properly in the hole before leaving the putting green and strictly observe legal notices regulating the movement of golf carts.

Scoring

There are a number of scoring systems used in golf, but the most common are stroke play, match play, stableford and bogey. You can play these on an individual or betterball basis where two people play as partners.

Stroke play

On stroke play, also known as medal play, the total number of times you strike the ball during a round, including penalty shots, is called your gross score. You then deduct your handicap from this score to determine your nett score. Most club competitions are decided on the nett score, enabling all players to compete, regardless of their handicaps.

Your handicap is determined by your playing ability, and is adjusted on a regular basis, depending on your form over the last 10 rounds or so. The maximum handicap allowed for men is usually 24, and 36 for women. A beginner will usually play off the maximum handicap and this will then be reduced as he improves down to scratch, or zero for the best golfers.

The par is considered to be the score a scratch player should make on that hole. On a par-three the scratch player would be expected to reach the green with one shot and then have two putts to complete the hole in three strokes. On a par-four he would be expected to reach the green with two shots and two putts will give him a par. On a par-five he would require three shots to get the ball to the green and two putts will give him a score of five, or par.

➲ *A golf course consists of 18 holes, usually made up of four par-threes, four par-fives and 10 par-fours, making par for the course 72.*

A golfer with a handicap of 18 would be expected to have a total score for the round of 18 over par, or 90. This equates to scoring one over par on each hole. If the scratch player scores a gross of 72 and the 18-handicapper scores a gross of 90, after deducting their handicaps they will both have the same nett score: 72.

If a golfer gets the ball onto the green with one shot on a par-three and has only one putt, to give a total of two, this will be one under par for that hole, known as a birdie. Scoring three on a par-four or four on a par-five is a birdie.

'Bogey' is when the score is one over par for the hole, such as a four on a par-three or a five on a par-four. A score of two-under par for the hole is an 'eagle', such as a two on a par-four or three on a par-five.

Matchplay

Matchplay is the term used when the winner is not decided by the total number of strokes played during the round, but on a hole-by-hole basis.

For a scratch golfer, the gross and nett score are the same. An 18-handicap golfer will be able to deduct one shot off his gross score on each hole to determine his nett score. The nett score will determine the winner of each hole. The player winning the most holes during the round will win the match.

Stableford

Here the golfer is awarded points on each hole, depending on his nett score for that hole. A nett par gives him two points, a nett birdie gives him three

points and a nett bogey, or one over par, gives him one point. A nett eagle, or two-under par will give him four points.

The points are then totalled at the completion of the round and the player with the most points wins the competition. A total score of 36 points indicates that a golfer has played exactly to his handicap.

Bogey

In a bogey competition the golfer plays for 'plus', 'minus' or zero on each hole depending on his score. A nett score of par will give him a zero, a nett bogey or one-over will give him a minus and a nett birdie will give him a 'plus'. A total score of zero will show that the golfer played to his handicap.

These can all be played on an individual or better-ball basis. At times all four players in the group will play as a team, and compete against the other groups in the field. This is known as an alliance competition.

There are variations on these forms of competition and they vary slightly from country to country and even from one club to another.

➲ Playing on a betterball basis – where two people play as partners against a competing team – can be incredibly rewarding particularly in the light of a shared victory.

Glossary

Birdie: When you get onto a green in regulation with two shots on a par four, for instance, and you need only one putt to get the ball in the hole. You would have hit the ball three times, or one under par. This is a birdie.

Blades: Heads of irons that don't have cavity backs.

Bogey: If you hit the ball one more time than the par of the hole you will score a bogey or one over par. A double bogey is when a player scores a five on a par-three, a six on a par-four or a seven on a par-five.

Break: The amount the ball turns, or moves left or right when putting is called the break of the putt. The line of your putt will depend on the break.

Bunker: A section of the course that has been dug out and filled with sand. Also known as a sand hazard.

Cavity backs: Most irons have a cavity at the back of the head to spread the weight of the club to the perimeter of the head.

Divot: The chunk of grass that you dig out of the fairway when trying to hit the ball.

Driver: A No. 1 wood made out of metal.

Dropping: There are situations where you need to lift the ball and drop it nearby. With some there might be a penalty shot involved and with others not. You must hold the ball at shoulder height when dropping it with your arm outstretched in front of you.

Fade: Basically a small slice, when the ball curves to the right, but perhaps 5yds (5m) or less (*see* p25).

Fairway: The closely cut area of grass between the tee and the green. This is where your first shot, or tee shot should land.

Fat shot: Where the club hits the ground before it gets to the ball.

Free drop: When you can drop the ball away from an obstacle without adding a penalty shot to your score.

Green: The area of very short grass at the end of the fairway. The hole into which you are trying to get the ball is cut into the green. It usually has a flag in it to show you where it is.

Gross score: The number of times you actually hit the ball, including penalty shots.

GUR: Ground under repair. Areas on the course where repair work or maintenance is taking place. Here a free drop is allowed.

Handicap: Having played 10 rounds, your average score for those rounds might be 82. If the par of the course is 72, this would mean your average score is 10 over par. This would then mean your handicap should be 10. If your average score over 10 rounds is 75 on a course with a par of 70, it would mean your handicap should be 5. Now two golfers can play, and by adjusting the scores by means of the handicaps, both have an equal chance of winning. Golf is one of the few sports where a beginner can play against the club champion, and both can enjoy the game.

Honour: The player, or team that had the best score on the previous hole gets to play first on the next hole.

Hook: This is when the ball goes to the left of the target and turns in the air.

Irons: Clubs with solid metal heads.

Lie: The angle of the sole of the club in relation to the shaft.

Loft: The angle of the clubface in relation to the ground.

Marker 1: A coin or similar object that you place behind the ball when you are allowed to lift it.

Marker, or scorer: A golfer playing in the same group as you, who will record your score on the scorecard, or 'mark' your scorecard.

Nett score: Your score after you have deducted your handicap.

Over the top: The term used when your right shoulder is too high on the downswing and your hands and arms swing outwards, getting the club to approach the ball from outside the target line. This is probably the most common fault in the game and is caused by right-side domination.

Par: Each hole has a par. A short hole is designed so that you can reach it with one shot from the tee. With two putts you would score three. This would be a par three. A par four would be a hole where a good golfer can reach the green with two shots, one from the tee and the next from the fairway. Two putts will give you a four, or par. A par five usually requires three shots to reach the green in regulation.

Peg: A little plastic or wooden object used on the tee to raise the ball off the ground.

Pitch mark: An indentation left by the landing of the ball on the green. If this is not fixed within a few minutes, that patch of grass will die.

Placing: A local rule implemented mostly during winter, where you are allowed to 'place' the ball one club-length nearer the hole.

Pull: The ball goes left, but flies in a straight line.

Push: The ball goes to the right, but flies in a straight line.

Putter: The club used on the green. It is shaped differently to the other clubs.

Rough: The longer grass surrounding the fairway.

Shank: A shot where the neck of the club – where the shaft is connected to the head – hits the ball to the right of the target.

Sky shot: A shot played with a wood, where the clubhead slices under the ball. This causes the ball to be struck with the top edge of the club and fly a lot higher than it is meant to, literally 'into the sky'.

Slice: The term used when the ball curves to the right of the target.

Soft spikes: Most clubs will not allow shoes with metal spikes. and soft spikes made of plastic or rubber are recommended instead.

Tee, or teeing ground: A designated area from where you must hit the first shot on each hole.

Thin shot: A shot where the club strikes the centre of the ball instead of the bottom of it, and the ball flies lower than it should.

Woods: The longest clubs in the bag. They are no longer made of wood, and today have hollow metal heads instead.

Associations

United Kingdom

- The R&A, St Andrews

  Fife

  Scotland

  KY 169JD

  United Kingdom

  Tel: +44 1334 460000

  Fax: +44 1334 460001

  Website: www.randa.org

United States of America

- United States Golf Association

  Website: www.usga.org

Canada

- Royal Canadian Golf Association

  Website: www.rcga.org

Australia

- Australian Golf Union

  153–155 Cecil Street

  South Melbourne VIC

  Australia

  3205

  Tel: +61 3 9699 7944

  Fax: +61 3 9690 8510

  Website: www.agu.org.au

New Zealand

- New Zealand Golf Association

  Level 1, Xacta Tower,

  94 Dixon Street.

  PO Box 11842

  Wellington

  New Zealand

  Tel: +64 4 385 4330

  Fax: +64 4 385 4331

  Website: www.nzga.co.nz

South Africa

- South African Golf Association

  Website: www.saga.co.za

Index

Italics represent photographs

Photographic credits

All location photography from Julian Fuhrmann and studio photography from André Wepener (Digital Images Solutions) except for those supplied by photographers or agencies as listed below:

Cover	Paul Hofman/Touchline
p2	Gallo Images/Getty Images
p4	Snapstock: Superstock
p6	Gallo Images/Getty Images
p8	Getty Images/Touchline Photo
p9	Gallo Images/Getty Images
p13	Imagestate/Photo Access
p35	Profimedia/Touchline Photo
p39	Gallo Images/Getty Images
p50	Profimedia/Touchline Photo
p51	Getty Images/Touchline Photo
p52	Profimedia/Touchline Photo
p54	Gallo Images/Getty Images
p55	Imagestate/Photo Access
p63	Images of Africa (www.imagesofafrica.co.za)
p64	Gallo Images/Getty Images
p65	Getty Images/Touchline Photo
p66	Tertius Pickard/Touchline Photo
p68	Giovani Simeone/Sime/Photo Access
p73	Gallo Images/Getty Images
p82	Images of Africa (www.imagesofafrica.co.za)
p86	Allsport Concepts/Touchline Photo
p87	Gallo Images/Getty Images
p103	Snapstock: Creasource
p111	Getty Images/Touchline Photo
p113	Images of Africa (www.imagesofafrica.co.za)
p114	Gallo Images/Getty Images
p117	Hans-Peter Huber/Sime/Photo Access
p119	Gallo Images/Getty Images
p120	Gallo Images/Getty Images

Acknowledgements

The publisher would like to thank John Thomson, manager of the Parow Golf Club in Cape Town for the use of his golf course and facilities. Also a special thanks to our models: Cameron Johnston, Carli Marais and Hugo Malan for their invaluable contribution to the shoot and who, in particular, exhibited an outstanding level of professionalism and patience on the day.